ROUTLEDGE LIBRARY EDITIONS: SOCIAL THEORY

Volume 87

TESTAMENT FOR SOCIAL SCIENCE

TESTAMENT FOR SOCIAL SCIENCE
An Essay in the Application of Scientific Method to Human Problems

BARBARA WOOTTON

LONDON AND NEW YORK

First published 1950 by Routledge

2 Park Square, Milton Park, Abingdon, Oxon OX14 4RN
711 Third Avenue, New York, NY 10017, USA

Routledge is an imprint of the Taylor & Francis Group, an informa business

First issued in paperback 2016

Copyright © 1950 George Allen & Unwin Ltd

All rights reserved. No part of this book may be reprinted or reproduced or utilised in any form or by any electronic, mechanical, or other means, now known or hereafter invented, including photocopying and recording, or in any information storage or retrieval system, without permission in writing from the publishers.

Notice:
Product or corporate names may be trademarks or registered trademarks, and are used only for identification and explanation without intent to infringe.

British Library Cataloguing in Publication Data
A catalogue record for this book is available from the British Library

ISBN: 978-0-415-72731-0 (Set)
ISBN: 978-1-138-79047-6 (Volume 87) (hbk)
ISBN: 978-1-138-98870-5 (Volume 87) (pbk)

Publisher's Note
The publisher has gone to great lengths to ensure the quality of this reprint but points out that some imperfections in the original copies may be apparent.

Disclaimer
The publisher has made every effort to trace copyright holders and would welcome correspondence from those they have been unable to trace.

TESTAMENT
FOR
SOCIAL SCIENCE

An Essay in the Application of
Scientific Method
to Human Problems

by
BARBARA WOOTTON

London
GEORGE ALLEN & UNWIN LTD
Ruskin House Museum Street

FIRST PUBLISHED IN 1950

This book is copyright under the Berne Convention. No portion may be reproduced by any process without written permission. Inquiries should be addressed to the publishers.

PRINTED IN GREAT BRITAIN
in 12-*pt. Bembo type*
BY THE BLACKFRIARS PRESS LTD.
SMITH-DORRIEN ROAD, LEICESTER

PREFACE

ANYONE who sets out to enquire into the possible contribution of scientific method to human problems needs to be equipped, if he is to discharge the task adequately, with wide expert knowledge in both natural and social science, and at least to be able to meet the philosophers on their own ground. I am acutely conscious that these qualifications are not mine. On many of the subjects discussed in these pages I write frankly as an amateur, though naturally I have done my best to become as well-informed an amateur as I can. Unfortunately, those who have sufficient *expertise* are few, and greatly occupied with their own specialisms. Failing their contribution, the impact of scientific research as a whole upon human life is best perhaps considered independently by both the social and the natural scientists from their respective viewpoints.

I am also well aware that on topics where no final certainty is yet possible—particularly those discussed in Chapters V, VI, and VII—alternative answers are possible to those which I have suggested. I did at one stage consider setting out the reasons why I in my turn reject the solutions which others will doubtless in some cases prefer : but the effect could only have been to make the argument impossibly cumbrous, and to obscure the main line of thought. I have therefore confined myself to setting out as fairly as I can the evidence for my own hypotheses, including the weak as well as the strong points, and leaving it at that—only asking that those who have answers to my answers to these questions should have in mind that there are also answers to theirs.

Throughout, I have given a good deal of space to the educational and academic implications of my thesis. This is partly because universities are the places where many (though not, of course, all) new discoveries are made ; and partly for the purely personal reason that these implications necessarily obtrude themselves upon anyone who has been much engaged in various forms of university education.

My indebtedness to a great stream of thought will be obvious enough. Some of what is written here is, I hope, original ; but much, of course, is not. You will find it in Mill, perhaps, or Comte or Bentham. There comes a time, however, when such debts can no longer be itemised : I know that I have drawn many buckets from the river, but I cannot hope to distinguish the water that has come from particular tributaries. More specific acknowledgements I am glad to be able to make—notably to several groups of undergraduate students, who set the main train of thought in motion, and were lively aids to its progress : to my colleagues, Professor H. B. Acton and Professor H. T. Flint, who were good enough to conduct a search for blunders in an earlier version of Chapter II : to W. B. Curry for a similar but more comprehensive review: and to Barbara Kyle for detecting many confusions of thought and obscurities of expression which had escaped my notice. For whatever mistakes remain, I alone, of course, am responsible.

B.W.

CONTENTS

PREFACE

		page
I.	*Introduction*	1
II.	*Scientific Method in the Social Sciences*	6
III.	*Pre-Scientific Mental Habits*	47
IV.	*Two Blind Alleys*	71
V.	*Science and Metaphysics*	93
VI.	*Science and Morals*	119
VII.	*Science and the Arts*	160
VIII.	*Conclusion*	178
	Index	193

★

CHAPTER ONE

INTRODUCTION

THE contrast between man's amazing ability to manipulate his material environment and his pitiful incompetence in managing his own affairs is now as commonplace as it is tragic. The world of atomic energy and nylon is for millions still the world of poverty, hunger, misgovernment, crime, domestic unhappiness or personal frustration. And mastery over earth and air and sea and atom has brought us only to daily fear of sudden death of our own making.

No one has any doubt how that mastery has been won. It is by rigorous devotion to scientific method that we have made our conquests over the material environment. Nor are we troubled by doubts as to the validity of the results which scientific research has thus achieved in the understanding of, and the consequent power to manipulate, inanimate things. The Christian and the Muslim, the Fascist and the Liberal, the idealist and the logical positivist may dispute endlessly about their views on human life and the nature of things; but they all accept the facts that steam engines will pull trains and amplifiers make their speeches more widely heard. Even the most primitive peoples quickly learn to put their trust in firearms.

It is no less obvious that this method, which has been so brilliantly successful in the natural sciences, is not normally applied to the field of our most disastrous failures. The personal relations of human beings, individual and collective, are conducted in a quite different way: these are for the most part governed by a medley of primitive impulses, kindly or harsh, sometimes even noble, modified by rules of thumb, and set in the framework of a traditional morality which varies from place to place and from age to age. In these matters science plays little part and commands but meagre respect. It may be true that of recent years the findings of the psychologists—often in seriously distorted versions—have begun to seep into this area of experience, affecting the personal relationships of individuals and the upbringing of children quite considerably, penal codes and practice somewhat less noticeably, national politics still less, and international politics hardly at all.[1] In these developments, as also in the growing prestige of empirical economic science, and in the gradual influence of anthropology upon the dealings of one cultural group with another, we may perhaps discern the beginnings of a very different future. But these are marginal occurrences: they have still not seriously modified the division of experience into two sharply divided sections—that in which science speaks with authority, and that in which she whispers furtively, or is dumb.

This contrast surely seems to point a simple moral—that we ought seriously to ask whether the tool that has worked such wonders in the one job could not be used for the other. More than a century has passed since Auguste Comte said that the rational reform of society must be brought about by the application of scientific method to social problems. If not very much has happened since to prove him right, certainly even less has happened to prove him wrong. In the intervening century scientific method has marched from victory to victory in the field of natural phenomena, while those human problems which have not enjoyed its attentions remain as intractable as ever.

It is, therefore, the first purpose of this essay to ask how far these problems also might be tackled by the methods of science. This is not, indeed, a simple matter; for scientific method is no magic formula whose incantation will perform any trick that may be desired. Certainly there are, at least in the present state of knowledge, real differences between the material to be handled by the

---

[1] though the study of International Tensions initiated by UNESCO may be a most significant omen here: and not less so, if some of its early projects look pretentious or over-ambitious.

INTRODUCTION

social and the natural sciences respectively. Human bodies may be bundles of atoms, but men and women are not atoms ; and their behaviour may, as we shall see, prove in some respects even more disorderly than that of the particles of which they are composed.

Nevertheless, as I hope to show, the potential contribution of science in this field is far greater than anything we have yet seen : the differences between the material of the social and the natural sciences are differences of degree, rather than of kind ; and even these are easily exaggerated. And the rewards of success are inestimable. Every fresh advance in the natural sciences—at least in physics, chemistry and bacteriology—now widens the gap between our material success and our social failure, and endangers still further the hope of happiness and civilised living, if not of actual survival, for the majority of mankind. That gap could be closed if, in the perspective of history, the age that lies before us could be as memorable in the social, as the nineteenth and twentieth centuries are already in the natural, sciences.

There are secondary rewards also. Our lives are darkened not only by the familiar threats, if not the actualities, of poverty, unemployment, famine, war, and all their attendant miseries and cruelties. Most of us also live under the clouds of one or other form of superstition ; and the dignity of our species is diminished by the gods and idols that we have created in our own image. The scientific method, which has enabled us to master our material environment, might dissipate those clouds also : for, while there may be questions which science cannot answer, yet a scientific approach to life enables us to face the universe both with greater realism and with a new sense of dignity and independence. And, finally, science may have far more to contribute than we yet realise towards the enrichment of the emotional and aesthetic experiences which are among the greatest delights of that peculiar organ of our species—the mind.

The consistency of the scientific approach to all the problems that concern us is, indeed, the underlying theme of this book. Science has already reshaped our material environment from top to bottom, and now stands ready, I suggest, to take up with equal zest, and we may fairly hope with hardly less effectiveness, the task of unravelling the tangled complexities of our own relationships. But the conquest of even the physical environment was not achieved without long and bitter battles against ancient superstitions. In the social sciences, where moral problems inevitably arise early and often, the scientist is bound to consider the repercussions of his work upon his whole philosophy ; and to chafe under the limitations imposed by any attempt to divide experience into the kingdom of dogma and the territory of science. That is why any review of the possibilities of scientific method as an instrument for handling the immediate practical perplexities of our social relationships leads inevitably into a discussion of the relation of science to metaphysics, morals and religion. The impact of the social sciences upon what is left of traditional religious doctrine has barely begun to be noticed. When its full vigour is felt, the resulting disturbance is likely to be hardly less violent than that created by the natural scientists of the nineteenth century.

Meanwhile, time presses. Measured by the perspective of our own age the progress of the natural sciences looks amazingly rapid : the bulk of it has been crowded into a couple of centuries. But, seen against the time-scale of all human history, the pace looks rather different. Moreover, we have to recognise that, so far as social science is concerned, we are still mostly living in the dark ages—at a level of sophistication hardly higher than that which primitive peoples, who see rocks and rivers as the dwelling-place of spirits, have attained in the corresponding sphere of the natural sciences. Certainly we cannot now be confident of moving fast enough to avoid disaster. The forces that make for wholesale destruction, mental and physical, in the contemporary world may well be gaining on us ; and compared with their velocity, the pace of even the most spectacular researches is alarmingly slow. For it is not only a case of waiting on the labours of a few thousands of professional investigators. What is no less necessary, and much more slowly come by, is a revolution in the mental attitude

INTRODUCTION

of the public. Even the natural sciences could not have borne practical fruit, had not the layman been prepared to respect, and indeed himself to use, the methods of science. In the social sciences his co-operation has still to be won.

Certainly, a scientific approach to social problems is no short cut. It is, however, no argument in favour of the wrong road to say that it is a short one. The risk that we may perish before we have travelled far enough is a reason for pushing ahead as fast as we can along the right track : not for taking short cuts that lead only to dead end or disaster.

CHAPTER TWO

SCIENTIFIC METHOD IN THE SOCIAL SCIENCES[1]

I

THE stages of the scientific process are now generally familiar. There is first the accurate observation of data; then the formulation of an hypothesis; and finally the promotion of the hypothesis by empirical verification to the status of a law. Scientific method 'is simply the attempt to acquire knowledge of general laws directly or indirectly by experience, by the use of our five senses.'[2] Our problem is thus to determine how far a parallel attempt can be made to acquire knowledge about human relationships.

To begin with the data: as the foregoing quotation implies, the data of the natural sciences are sensory observations. The elaborate and often abstract structures which the scientist builds from his material may seem far removed from this homely foundation; yet all science begins (and for that matter ends, since sensory confirmation is always necessary for final proof) in things that are seen or heard, smelt, tasted or touched. There are, indeed, acute philosophical controversies as to the significance of this sense-

---

[1]Throughout this book I use the terms 'social studies' and 'social science' to cover the whole field of enquiries relating to man's behaviour and activities. Psychology, history and anthropology, as well as ethics and aesthetics, are thus included in the social sciences, in contrast to non-human natural sciences such as physics and chemistry. Subjects like biology and medicine cut across this classification. Since the amenability of these to the ordinary tools of scientific method is not generally disputed, it is convenient for the particular purposes of this book to include them with the natural sciences. It is in any case not necessary to draw precise lines. I am only concerned to consider how far the methods employed in what are accepted as the natural sciences can be fruitful in the distinctively human fields in which their status is at present unestablished. The use of 'social' in this context as virtually synonymous with 'human' is not intended to exclude studies of, say, individual psychology. Admittedly such a usage is difficult to justify etymologically; but I hope that it may pass on grounds of convenience, especially as nothing in this terminology in any way affects the argument of the book.

[2]*Scientific Method* by A. D. Ritchie (Kegan Paul), p. 189.

experience, and as to the measure in which we are justified in describing the phenomena that our senses present to us and the constructs that science makes of these as 'real'. These controversies can, however, be ignored in the present context, since our task is not to discuss the metaphysical status of scientific discoveries but, rather, to ask how far the processes of science, whatever their status, can be transferred to human affairs. Doubts whether scientific discoveries are anything more than thoughts in the minds of scientists cannot greatly have consoled the people of Hiroshima on 6th August 1945. In the present enquiry, where they would be disturbing rather than consolatory, they can for the most part also be neglected : we can accept the common view that if you can see a brick wall or walk into it in the dark, that is good enough evidence that the wall is there.

It is, however, relevant to the later argument of this book to note that there are two special reasons[1] for treating what we like to call the evidence of our senses with particular respect. The first is the irresistible nature of the experience : except by obstructing the sense organs involved, it is impossible to escape sensory experience, given an appropriate stimulus. Unless you shut your eyes or obstruct your nose, you must see or smell whatever is there to be seen or smelt. The second reason is the almost universal agreement amongst human beings that sensory experience *is* valid evidence of objective reality. This agreement is, significantly, independent of cultural level, nor does it have to be deliberately implanted in the young. The sophisticated man of science and the simplest primitive both act upon the presumed truth of our assumption about a brick wall.[2] For these reasons the data supplied by the senses are often described as 'primary' or even 'brute', or, to use Professor Ritchie's more picturesque phrase, 'primitive'.

---

[1] I am much indebted to Norman Campbell's book *What is Science?* (Methuen) for the method of presentation used in this chapter. As a popular exposition, this book, though now nearly thirty years old, has never been surpassed.

[2] I have ventured to omit discussion of the age-long problem about the reality of the sense-experience of highly intoxicated persons who assert that they see pink elephants which are not visible to their neighbours; because these and similar problems, though important in themselves, take us further into philosophy than is necessary for our limited purpose.

So far, so good; for much of the data of the social sciences is exactly the same. Mr. Vishinsky shaking his head at Lake Success is visible to the eye : the crowd at a political meeting is perceived by eye and ear. Types of behaviour which are classified as 'crime' or 'aggression' are perceptible only by the senses (though their classification as such naturally brings in other factors). The victim who is assaulted by a criminal becomes aware of the fact through his sense of touch and perhaps also by sight : aggressive behaviour means physical actions like letting off bombs, or, on a milder scale, giving vent to cross words or looks. Even so abstract a concept as mental cruelty can only be perceived through its expression in speech or actions which impinge upon the senses. In short, our knowledge about the behaviour of other people, just like our knowledge of the phenomena studied by the natural sciences, is ordinarily finally derived from 'brute' or 'primitive' sense perceptions.

Even the social scientist who is occupied with the study of what are called institutions must draw his ultimate data (with one important exception discussed below) from the experience of the senses. Suppose, for instance, that he is engaged on a study of the rôle of trade unions in contemporary England. The abstract conception 'trade union' is simply shorthand for certain types of behaviour by certain people, of which we can only be aware by sensory perception. It means men sitting in a room and making certain sounds in the conduct of a 'trade union meeting', or handing over to other persons tangible objects (money) as their subscriptions to the union. Anyone who wishes to make a study of trade unions, or even of the more abstract conception 'trade unionism', can only do so either by personally observing such behaviour, or by using his eyes and ears on books and speeches made by other people who have themselves made such observations (or who have in their turn heard or seen records of such observations made by others). Even such comments on a union meeting as that it was 'orderly' or 'peaceful' are fundamentally statements about its physical properties : an orderly meeting is presumably one in which people do not make noises by banging upon the table or speaking very loudly.

This dependence of social studies upon sense perceptions is certainly a wholesome reminder of the fundamental homogeneity of the original data of science. For knowledge of the external world, whether of things or of people, we continually come back to our five senses in the end. Nevertheless, if a great mass of data relevant to social science is sensory, we have, I think, also to admit an important collection that is not—namely, the whole body of primary mental or psychological experience. Perception of mental pleasure and pain appears to have the same universality as sensory experience. At all levels of culture, sensations of simple happiness and unhappiness are as general as are the experiences of seeing and hearing. It is of course true that no person can experience the feelings of anyone other than himself; but equally no one can see with another's eyes or hear with another's ears. The grounds for belief in the sense experiences of other people and the grounds for belief in their primitive psychological experiences are thus both equally shaky, or equally firm. We derive our conviction that other people experience emotion from the fact that they say so, and from analogies between their behaviour and our own: we derive our conviction that they see and hear from exactly the same evidence.

The irresistibility of psychological experience is perhaps slightly more disputable. If one's eyes are open and one looks in a certain quarter, one cannot help seeing. Is it equally true that one cannot help a feeling of pleasure or pain or shock or excitement? Essentially, I should say that it is. But it is clear that primitive emotional reactions can be inhibited: one can, for example, contrive not to be depressed by an event. Nevertheless, if we stand back from all philosophical niceties and ask ourselves whether psychological sensation ought to be omitted from the data of the social sciences on the ground that it is doubtfully 'primitive', there cannot, I think, be much doubt about the answer. We must conclude with Bertrand Russell 'that there is knowledge of private data, and that there is no reason why there should not be a science of them.'[1] Equally, if we consider whether the similarities or the differences, in this matter of universality-plus-irresistibility, between psychological and sensory experience are the more impressive, we are surely bound to come down on the side of the similarities. Certainly, social studies which consistently ignored human feelings would be worse than laughable.

This still leaves all the phenomena of supposedly unconscious mental processes to be accounted for. But these cannot, I think, claim to rank as primitive experience. The evidence for their existence is, for one thing, quite different from that by which the universality of sensory perception is commended to our common sense. Since by definition you cannot be conscious of what goes on in your unconscious mind, you cannot, by analogy, infer that there are similar goings-on in the unconscious mind of anybody else. Unconscious processes, in fact, cannot be reckoned as part of experience at all, since nobody experiences them. It follows that theories about the unconscious must rank as hypotheses (and metaphorical ones at that) designed to 'explain' the primitive experience known as sensory and emotional perception, and not as part of that experience. As such, they could, in fact be abandoned without damage to the whole structure of scientific knowledge, should later evidence, checked by reference to genuinely primitive experience, so require ; whereas to discard the basic data of primitive perceptions would mean giving up the whole attempt to make sense of the world, and would cut at the root of every science. It is indeed possible, though not, perhaps, very likely, that we shall some day cease to believe in the unconscious, as the physicists have ceased to believe in the ether. This will not shatter psychology any more than physics was shattered by the disappearance of the ether. But both would collapse if we ceased to accept the evidence of our own eyes, and abandoned the distinction between happiness and misery.

In the natural sciences, the importance of accurate observation

---

[1] *Human Knowledge* (George Allen & Unwin), p. 62.

of primary data needs no emphasis. The natural scientist knows well enough that he must record exactly what he sees and not what he expected to see, or what he wanted to see : nor even what he would have seen had he not been looking elsewhere. He knows also that his observation must be strictly primary : he must not confuse inferences of his own with the simple facts of what his senses have perceived, though here, indeed, is a line which is easily crossed unawares. For the 'pure bruteness of experience . . . has never been entertained by anyone . . . no sensation has ever taken place without some kind of minimal judgment. We cannot see red without the idea of redness or the understanding of something red.'[1]

Furthermore, if the scientist's observation is not to remain merely his private experience, he must make an accurate recording of what he has observed. In order to achieve the precision necessary for that purpose, very good use has been made of dead languages. By coining technical terms from Latin and Greek words not used outside their specialised scientific context in any contemporary language, scientists have eliminated the necessity of defining any term more than once, or the risk that by association the same word will convey different meanings to different people. The fact that by this means they have also provided themselves with an international language is an incidental, but not unimportant, advantage.

In the social sciences both observation and description present some special difficulties. There is not, indeed, any problem arising from scarcity or inaccessibility of data. We are, on the contrary, blessed with a superabundance of raw material : it lies all around us on the doorstep of everyday life. It is rather the very familiarity of the material which makes it difficult to establish accurate observations. The various situations of family life, or the ingredients in social and political problems, are so much matters of everyday experience that we have long since ceased to notice

---

[1] *What Science Really Means* by Julius W. Friend and James Feibleman (George Allen & Unwin), p. 123.

them. In consequence, we are likely to miss the actual facts and substitute for them mental stereotypes of our own. It is, indeed, no accident that anthropology—a science whose range is by definition as wide as humanity—never begins at home : remoter data are more easily seen in perspective. Only when anthropological science has reached a relatively mature level of self-consciousness, does it venture to turn its interest towards the habits and institutions of its own practitioners.

Meanwhile, the difficulties in the way of accurate observation of social phenomena should make us grateful to the behaviourist psychologists and the social anthropologists who have troubled to record the facts of human behaviour with precision and detail. Such observations are the foundation upon which alone valid inference in great tracts of human affairs can be made. If some of them appear aimless and tedious, that, at the present embryo stage of social enquiry, is only what is to be expected ; and it is a small price to pay for the fruitful generalisations that may emerge from those observations that are more happily selected. After all, precise recordings of human behaviour have only been attempted in very recent times. 'Mankind has thrown away most of its experience for lack of competent record-making, and successive generations are left with a more meagre social inheritance than need be.'[1]

In the social sciences, moreover, the temptation to be careless about distinguishing primary perception from secondary inference is exceptionally severe ; and, again, the chief reason is that the inferences are themselves so much matters of common experience that their indirect origin is long forgotten. The social investigator in the example of the trade union used above is inclined to treat the distinction between a peaceful and a disorderly meeting as a matter of immediate perception. The very fact that his first-line inferences are concepts in popular use (including popular speech) tends to make him forget that they *are* still inferences ; and vague

---

[1] *The Analysis of Political Behaviour* by Harold Lasswell (Kegan Paul), p. 9.

ones at that. In common usage such terms as 'peaceful' and 'disorderly' have no precision ; and two observers of the same meeting may adjudge it in these terms quite differently.

The remedy is a keen recognition of inference for what it is, coupled with the utmost precision in definition of terms. On that matter also, however, the social scientists are far behind their colleagues in physics or chemistry or medicine. The task of translating private observations into public information *need* not present greater difficulties in social than in natural science ; but at the moment it does ; for the social sciences have still not equipped themselves with an adequate technical vocabulary. They have refrained from doing this largely, I think, from timidity. Both natural and social sciences in the first instance address themselves to data which are within the range of ordinary human experience. The natural sciences, however, proceed to manipulate these data in ways which take them far beyond those limits. In the course of these operations they can use what language they please, and no one will care, because at this stage they are moving in a private world of their own. The layman does not expect to understand what goes on in a physical or even a pathological laboratory, and suffers no humiliation if he is ignorant of the language used in these places. Only the results of these mysteries, as distinct from the mysteries themselves, are likely to come within his experience —in the hospital ward perhaps, or on the battlefield,—and for the discussion of these no special vocabulary may be necessary.

The social sciences, on the other hand, are much more apt to conduct all their business in the market place ; and the use of technical terms for this purpose tempts the public to deride them for their addiction to jargon. On this account (and partly also, it is fair to say, from an admirable dislike of obscurity for obscurity's sake) the social scientists have unnecessarily and unwisely deprived themselves of valuable tools ; though the Americans have tended in this matter to live up to their reputation for self-confidence, and shown themselves on the whole less sensitive to such ridicule than their colleagues on the other side of the Atlantic. In the absence of these tools, shift has to be made with clumsy substitutes. Such terms as 'nation', 'capitalism', 'problem-family', 'civilisation', 'democracy', 'investment', 'middle-class', must be defined afresh by each investigator who wishes to use them, and strictly confined in their use within the limits thus laid down ; while every reader's mind must be at once sufficiently adaptable and sufficiently precise for him to be able to divest himself of any personal verbal associations, and to switch from the definition employed by one writer to that chosen by another, using each in turn as though it were his own. In these conditions accuracy is not, indeed, impossible ; but the door is gratuitously opened to risks of error.[1]

II

From the business of observation, the scientist passes next to the task of formulating an hypothesis to 'explain' the phenomena that he has observed. The hypothesis will, of course, if only in the form of a vague 'hunch', already have influenced the selection of data to be examined. It could not be otherwise in view of the vast array of phenomena which enters into our experience. Even at the stage of observation, the student who is interested in the yield of different varieties of wheat takes note of such factors as rainfall and the properties of the soil in the area under observation, but is generally indifferent to statistics of infant mortality. By making this selection he is, of course, already committed to the hypothesis that rain and soil may affect his plants, while the deaths of young children will not.

The psychological processes that lead to a fruitful hypothesis are still quite obscure. The attitude of scientific men themselves on the subject is rather curious. They seem often strangely anxious to give the impression that it is a matter right outside the scope of scientific investigation. Reaching an hypothesis is, they say, an art, not a function of science ; which is only another way of asserting that it is a part of nature in which no order is to be found. Thus

---

[1] Of the consequences of laxity in the use of terms at a more popular level, I shall have more to say later. See Chap. III.

Professor Ritchie: 'it is quite impossible to lay down rules knowing which anybody can write poems like Shelley or make statues like Praxiteles. So also it is impossible to lay down rules which will enable anybody to make discoveries like Faraday and Pasteur.'[1] Dr. N. R. Campbell is also concerned to make the same point by his emphasis on the role of genius in science.[2] And Professor Ritchie is quite shocked at Bacon for having apparently thought otherwise. 'Impossible' is, however, a large word, especially from the pen of a man of science; and obscurantism about future scientific research is always rash. Investigation into the relationship between the brain and the mind and the psycho-physical processes which accompany flashes of insight whether in the arts or in scientific thought has barely begun, while study of the genetic and environmental factors responsible for the production and successful functioning of outstanding ability is not much further advanced. Enough, however, has already been achieved to make us at least cautious of belittling future possibilities. Bacon might yet have the last laugh.[3]

Whatever the mechanism which produces a useful hypothesis may be, there is clearly no reason to suppose that it differs according to whether the relevant data are drawn from the field of physical or social phenomena. The actual function of the hypothesis in the scientific process raises, however, rather more complex issues. The hypothesis itself is clearly enough an intelligent anticipation of scientific law; but the nature of the laws which science seeks thus to establish needs to be rather more closely examined, if we are to reach a clear view on the crucial question whether comparable laws can be formulated also in the social sciences. Both the hypothesis and the law itself are likely to be expressed in explanatory or causative terms. The agricultural investigator finds that a crop does badly *because* there is insufficient iron in the soil: that he says, *explains* its failure. Actually, however, this causative

---

[1] *Scientific Method*, p. 53.
[2] *What is Science?* especially pp. 72, 73.
[3] The matter is discussed more fully in connection with the subject of creative genius in the arts in Chap. VII.

explanatory business turns out, as will presently appear, to be a very slippery affair, and we shall be on safer ground if we confine ourselves to expressing the laws of science simply as statements of association between phenomena. If the phenomenon A is found to be consistently associated with the phenomenon B, we had better reserve judgment on such questions as whether A causes B, or B causes A, or both are caused by C. The generalised knowledge—that is the law—that we derive from observation of the data guided by the hypothesis, can be stated simply as the association of A with B.

Such associations may be invariable, in which case the law is disproved by a single instance, contradicting what it asserts ; or they may merely enjoy varying degrees of probability ; the former is, of course, simply a limiting case of the latter. The association, for example, of a given heat with the appearance of bubbles on the surface of water, that is the phenomenon known as boiling, appears to be invariable. On the other hand, the association of a black cloud overhead in the English climate with a downpour of rain is frequent, but not invariable.

Theoretically there are three possible reasons why in some cases we should only be able to assert the probability of an association, whereas in others we speak with complete confidence. The first is ignorance. Associations are often complex : the association of A with B, for instance, may be contingent on the absence of C ; and of that we may still be ignorant. A law, or, if you prefer, an approximation to a law, may, therefore, have only a low degree of probability, because, although we have established some of the relevant associations, others are still unknown. Again, in a particular instance, or in relation to a particular class of phenomena, adequate data may be lacking, to which laws of association already established can be applied. If I ask a meteorologist whether I should take my umbrella on a given occasion, the forecast on which his advice will be based may have a degree of probability lower than certainty for both these reasons. Even the expert does not know the exact state of the weather at the time, and if he did, he still may not be sure enough about the conditions that are invariably accompanied by rain to give a certain answer.

The third possible reason why statements of association should fall short of certainty is of an altogether different kind: it is that there may be regions in which consistent associations do not hold at all, and which are, therefore, outside the field of scientific enquiry altogether. This type of explanation has the attraction of putting the blame, so to speak, for the limitations of our knowledge upon the universe instead of upon ourselves; and it is perhaps for this reason that certain scientists in philosophers' clothing[1] occasionally exhibit a weakness for such doctrines. It is agreeable to think that what is unknown to us in our day and generation is also unknowable. The advance of knowledge has, however, constantly shown how false such an assumption might have been in the past: forewarned by this, we should be wise to presume that this assumption is not less dubious now. It is, moreover, a merit of the opposite presumption—that it is ignorance rather than absence of order which lowers the probability of our statements of association—that it may be proved right and can never be proved wrong: whereas an assumption of disorderliness may be proved wrong and cannot ever be proved right.

For our purpose, however, what matters is the *fact* that associations are of varying degrees of probability. Those who ascribe this to the inherent disorderliness of phenomena will naturally be more pessimistic about the prospects of further research; but since they cannot give any evidence for their pessimism, and since the optimists have so often turned out to be right in the past, we need not be overmuch disturbed by this. In practice what we call knowledge consists of a hierarchy of probable associations. As further discoveries are made, associations of lower probability are revised and promoted in their new form to higher rank; and additions are made to the list of certainties.

In reducing the laws of science to bald statements of association,

---

[1] Notably Sir James Jeans. See, for instance, *The Mysterious Universe* (Cambridge University Press) especially pp. 20, 21.

we have, it will be recalled, omitted all reference to cause and effect. There is, perhaps, something chilly and unsatisfactory about this: our minds hanker for something that looks more secure and comfortable—particularly for a mechanical concept of cause and effect. The heat we like to say *makes* the water boil: the nutriment in the soil *makes* the crops grow. Like many other comfortable notions the concept of cause and effect seems to have been particularly influential amongst the Victorians. To borrow an illuminating image of Dr. Bronowski's,[1] the nineteenth-century scientists imagined that the planets were 'caused to keep their orbits . . . by a kind of invisible celestial elastic'—known as the force of gravitation; and it is for this elastic that we crave insistently, as the missing link between associated phenomena.

Nevertheless, every attempt to establish the existence of this link in its own right founders inevitably. The elastic is as elusive as it is invisible: the order that we can perceive in the universe is not so much a matter of links and chains as simply an observed regularity of patterns. For the search for causal connections between associated phenomena simply resolves itself in turn into a long process of 'explaining' one association in terms of another. If a person becomes ill with what are known as diabetic symptoms, we measure the sugar-content of his blood. If this is higher than that found in people not exhibiting such symptoms, we say that the high sugar-content is the *cause* of the illness; which is only another way of saying that the two are linked by a law of association previously established. If we go further and ask why the diabetic has so much sugar in his blood, this in turn is said to be 'explained' by a failure of the pancreas to function normally, that is to say, by an observed association between a certain condition of the pancreas and the sugar-content of the blood. And so on, with one law of association following another, until we are at last stuck with something which we have not yet been able to associate consistently with anything else.

---

[1] From one of a Third Programme series of broadcasts, 16th April, 1948. I am indebted to Dr. Bronowski and to the British Broadcasting Corporation for kindly letting me see the unpublished text of this.

The function of the hypothesis, then, is simply to suggest laws of association. Before we turn to the social sciences, it will be useful to note that the hypothesis itself may be derived from deductive reasoning or inductive observation, or a mixture of both. The use of the deductive hypothesis is, to be sure, fraught with special dangers of its own. To quote Professor Ritchie again: 'We can, if we like, make classes by definition and find laws among them by deduction, but the result will not be scientific knowledge; it may possibly be pure mathematics but it is more likely to be pure nonsense.'[1]

On the other hand, deductive hypotheses can be extraordinarily valuable in suggesting where to look for previously undetected laws of association; and may lead the enquirer far beyond the phenomena to which his attention was first directed. Such hypotheses or 'theories' as they are sometimes called, in a special sense of that word, to some extent satisfy the hunger for explanation which seems to be so deep-seated in our minds. The Mendelian theory of inheritance, for example, offers an explanation of certain observed relations between the characters of parents and their offspring. If this hypothesis were true, its authors argued that, not only would they get the results actually observed by crossing tall sweet peas and short sweet peas: they would expect crossing of other varieties of animals and plants to show similar results in terms of the theory: which it did. The prestige of the theory was accordingly enhanced, and its scope has been continually enlarged by use of the same methods.

Theories of this kind take a number of forms. In physics they are apt to be mathematical: here it is logical deductions from mathematical propositions which put us on the track of hitherto unrealised associations. In other cases theories may be pictorial or metaphorical. At one stage atomic theory contained a considerable pictorial element: I recall a distinguished physical chemist who used to carry about in his pocket rubber models of the molecules which he had never seen, but which played a central part in his

---

[1] *Scientific Method*, p. 194.

theories. Metaphorical theories are, however, always dangerous inasmuch as the metaphor tends to divert attention from the actual phenomena under consideration to the imaginary concepts contained in the metaphor itself; and there is a certain temptation to read into the data associations which are appropriate only to the metaphor.

Finally, the search for hypotheses, like the selection of data, is itself guided by considerations of consistency with the pattern of already established associations. If a theory cuts across this, it will certainly be under suspicion. Many a possible hypothesis is weeded out, and not even allowed, so to speak, to sit the examination for empirical proof, because of its incredibility on this account. In the case of our diabetic patient, for example, the hypothesis that the condition of his pancreas is inherited, or due to malnutrition, might at some stage of research command respect, because an association between hereditary and nutritional factors in other diseases has been definitely established; but no one is likely to embark on enquiries designed to ascertain whether his illness is connected with the fact that his surname begins with P. On the other hand, this is readily accepted as the reason why a name always appears in the latter half of the telephone directory.

III

As soon as we set out to frame hypotheses in the hope of establishing parallel laws of association in the social sciences, we are met by the formidable allegation that human affairs are wholly intractable by this process or at least insufficiently tractable to make the effort worth while. Hence before we can discuss any special features of the search for hypotheses in this field, we have to take up this challenge to the very existence of the laws which every hypothesis seeks to anticipate. Clearly, if there are no laws, no hypothesis can anticipate them, and the attempt to frame such hypotheses is a waste of everybody's time.

The main grounds of this challenge appear to be as follows. First, it is argued that there is an indeterminacy inherent in human behaviour which precludes the formulation of any valid laws of association. Men and women, it is said, act incalculably, just as from time to time it may seem good to them to act. In terms of Dr. Bronowski's simile this might be called the argument from the missing elastic. It is an argument, however, which has lost most of its force, since the elastic disappeared also from the non-human world. So long as cause and effect were conceived in mechanical terms as a binding compulsion, with cause dragging effect relentlessly along on an invisible string, it was more difficult to formulate laws relating to human behaviour which did not reduce man also to a mechanically-operated contraption. The social scientist, therefore, looked like being forced very definitely to the determinist side of the controversy between necessity and freewill. Since, however, the conception of recurring regularities of pattern has ousted the mechanistic cause-and-effect idea as the basis of order in the non-human universe, we can safely leave open the question whether, and if so in what sense, the people of *Erewhon* were right in their belief that 'the most daring flight of the imagination or the most subtle exercise of the reason is as much the thing that must arise, and the only thing that can by any possibility arise, at the moment of its arising, as the falling of a dead leaf when the wind shakes it from the tree'.[1]

As we have seen, the laws of natural science are only statements of association of varying degrees of probability. If associations of comparable probability (or of any degree of probability higher than pure chance) can be demonstrated by observation to hold good of human affairs (as I hope to show that they can), then the meaning of law in both natural and social science is fundamentally the same. Moreover, we should do well to remind ourselves that the effects upon our generalisations of our own ignorance on the one hand, or of inherent disorderliness in our data on the other hand, would, as in the natural sciences, be identical. Both pull us down in the scale of probability; and no one can say whether lack of certainty means that no reliable associations exist, or that

---

[1] *Erewhon*, by Samuel Butler (Cape), pp. 256, 257.

associations are present but still undiscovered. And we should still further remind ourselves that the natural sciences, just as much as social science, would come to a dead stop, if we now decided to make the assumption that everything beyond the present frontiers of knowledge is devoid of regularities and therefore inaccessible to scientific method. Such an assumption would, of course, have been equally well warranted, if it had been made before the earliest beginnings of scientific investigations. To have acted upon it then would obviously have effectively prevented the accumulation of all our present scientific knowledge. It would be a disaster if a comparable defeatism were allowed to stultify the potentialities of scientific method in the relatively unexplored field of human affairs.

A second challenge to the possibility of formulating valid laws of association in human affairs stems from the complexity of the situations with which the social scientist has to deal, and the rarity of the cases in which effectively controlled experiment is possible. This is a real problem, but it is easily exaggerated. There are several reasons for facing it with optimism.

The first is the conspicuous fact that, even without any refined scientific technique, many valid generalisations about human behaviour are in fact constantly made. Civilised life, or indeed any social life at all, even at a quite primitive level, would be impossible without them. The baker can *generally* be relied on to bake, the postman to deliver the letter, and the addressee to be willing and able to read it. It would be safe to bet long odds that Aunt Mary will remember your birthday, and that Uncle Tom will bring any conversation round to himself. If none of these associations reaches the certainty of the statement that water will bubble and steam at a given temperature, all of them are much more often right than they would be if the matter were one of pure chance. And many of them have a higher degree of probability than have some of the more tentative associations established by recognised natural sciences. All of us can probably forecast in a limited number of specific situations the behaviour of a few people whom we know intimately with a degree of probability which, while it falls short of that with which astronomers foretell eclipses, yet easily surpasses the success with which the meteorologists prophesy tomorrow's weather in England. Certainly we do not lack hypotheses to explain our own or our neighbour's behaviour, even if the selection of data is differently weighted, and the relevant hypothesis differently framed, in the two cases. And if our generalisations about social behaviour do fail from time to time, it is arguable that our guesses make quite as good a showing in relation to the data as did our opinions about natural phenomena before these had been satisfactorily explained. We are probably making big mistakes about, say, the causes of war and the forms of government best adapted to our needs and natures. But it was also a big mistake to think that the sun went round the earth.

Secondly, the fact that possible associations can be established by crude observation should encourage the view that in the social, as in the natural, sciences, better observation would yield generalisations of a higher degree of probability. Here again, a sensible person conducts his ordinary life on this assumption. He does not argue that to make a small chance of being right into a larger one is not worth while in cases where one cannot hope to attain complete certainty. If you are particular about food and drink, and you propose to take a holiday in a place that you have not previously visited, you do not choose your hotel at random from the directory. You make such enquiries as you can from the hotels themselves; and, since in these matters experience has shown that independent evidence is of superior value, you will also, if you can, get advice from other people who know the place.

In this context, devotees of racing and of football pools should be a lesson to us. The data on which they have to work are generally such as only permit forecasts of very low probability. Nevertheless, thousands of enthusiasts study form with meticulous care in the hope of raising a small chance into one slightly larger. And where there is little to be gleaned from the actual data, they are eager to get all the help that they can from mathematical theory in choosing their permutations.

In any case, the complexity of the conditions to be unravelled in human problems varies greatly in different cases. We should do well to get ahead with those that are comparatively simple, the more so as these often turn out to be directly related to the other more complicated tasks. Psychology is the one human science that can to some extent avail itself of laboratory experiments, and can, therefore, study, under controlled conditions, certain carefully isolated aspects of human behaviour. In this way a body of knowledge is in process of being built up showing what human beings really are like. If the social scientists are not yet ready to make pronouncements on larger issues such as the psychological causes of war, let us remember that the physicists had to engage in most elaborate studies of minutiae before they could produce results that would blow up the world. Laboratory experiments, and nearlaboratory work such as the close observations of individuals made by psychiatrists, are beginning to enable us to classify temperaments, to measure intelligence, to distinguish between hereditary traits and those that are environmentally produced, and to map the conditions with which guilt and aggression are associated. Knowledge on these topics is the basis of understanding of the larger problems of, say, government and economic relationships, just as the work of the cultural anthropologists is the beginning of wisdom in international affairs.

Psychology is, indeed, so demonstrably the foundation of the social sciences that it is from many points of view to be regretted that these are not all regarded as branches of it. This is not just a matter of convenience of academic classification; for there is a real risk that other studies will go wrong because their psychology is false. In the absence of scientific knowledge based on accurate empirical observations, historians, economists and political theorists have worked on a few crude assumptions about human nature. They have, in consequence, only too often produced sweeping interpretations or intricate intellectual systems far removed from actuality. Man is neither wholly brutish and nasty, nor completely dominated by the economic calculus ; and he will not learn how to govern himself satisfactorily or to satisfy his bodily needs until he has a much clearer idea about the proportions in which these and other ingredients are compounded in his make-up, and the measure in which the mixture can be modified to taste.

The answer, then, to the challenge that social affairs are too complex to be susceptible of scientific treatment is threefold. In the first place, nothing more is involved by that challenge than an admission that we must for the present be content with fairly low degrees of probability ; though it would be unwise to prejudge the rate at which progress may be made to higher levels. Secondly, since we are all making generalisations anyhow, it is only common sense to get these as nearly accurate as possible; and, thirdly, the complexity of conditions and the impossibility of simplifying them by experiment is a much more formidable obstacle in some fields than in others ; and it is fortunate that the departments in which these obstacles are least terrifying are also those in which advance is most clearly a precondition of progress everywhere else. Meanwhile, whatever the measure of probability which the generalisations of social science have so far achieved, the generalisations themselves can only be reached by the same process as the laws of the natural sciences.

In the social, as in the natural sciences, the hypothesis which precedes the formulation of laws can be reached either by inductive or by deductive methods. In the social sciences, however, the use alike of inductive and of deductive reasoning has often been somewhat undisciplined.[1] In both cases this is no doubt a fault of infancy. In the field of economics in particular, deductive argument at one time showed a dangerous neglect of Professor Ritchie's warning[2] that the result of making classes by definition and finding laws among them by deduction 'may possibly be

---

[1] For a lively discussion of this whole subject see *Sociology at the Crossroads* (Longmans) by T. H. Marshall.

[2] See p. 19.

pure mathematics' but 'is more likely to be pure nonsense'. Certain economists seem to have believed that to Professor Ritchie's two classes, a third should be added, namely, pure economics. Having once peeped into the book of experience, these economists seem to have resolved never to open it again. Their one peep told them that human behaviour in industrial societies is significantly influenced by the prospect of economic advancement. By deduction from that premise and from that alone, they created elaborate structures without ever returning for empirical confirmation. The result looked suspiciously like a hybrid between Professor Ritchie's two classes. Happily, however, the phase in which economists were inclined to go crazy about deduction seems now to be passing.[1]

Amongst many sociologists, on the other hand, inductive methods have been more popular; but these in turn have often proved futile for lack of fruitful hypotheses to guide the selection of data. The blind accumulation of facts uninformed by any hypothetical interpretation of what is so industriously recorded is a barren enterprise; and it is particularly futile when the data themselves are already largely matters of common experience. A mere rearrangement or classification of what is already known is not in itself necessarily a significant addition to knowledge. But whatever effort may have been wasted in this way, the habit of noticing too much rather than too little is, after all, a fault on the right side. Particularly in the early stages of a science the exploration of blind alleys is to be expected; if you are completely lost, it is not a bad plan to try to make a note of nearly everything that you can see. After a time, something that makes sense may emerge from some region of what till then looked like complete confusion.

Hypotheses which take the form of metaphorical theories play a large part in the social sciences, as for instance in the conception of *libido*, conceived as a stream of undifferentiated psychic energy. And the dangers of metaphorical theories are probably greater in

---

[1] I have discussed this matter more fully in my *Lament for Economics* (George Allen & Unwin).

the social than in the natural sciences—particularly in those branches whose primary data is psychological rather than physical, for in these cases the metaphor is not easily checked back against hard factual observations. Once we have, for instance, imagined psychic energy in the form of a river, the possible developments of the metaphor are very alluring : the river can be dammed up, or diverted or forced underground. Obviously all these things may happen to a real river ; but one should be careful not to assume that, in consequence, they can in any meaningful sense happen also to an imaginary one in the human mind.

The final stage of the scientific process is reached when the hypothesis passes the test of empirical verification and is promoted to the rank of law. It is at this stage that the technique of controlled experiment has proved so valuable. Since nature does not often oblige us with the identical situations necessary for exact comparisons, we proceed to construct these artificially in the laboratory whenever we can. Even so, however, we need by no means despair of making any advances in knowledge at all in circumstances in which controlled experiment is precluded. We have, for instance, acquired a creditable knowledge of astronomy without being able as yet to make the stars dance to our tune. In this case it is no doubt a help that the relevant conditions are comparatively simple. But at the other end of the scale even the meteorologists are not deterred by the complexity of their data and the impossibility of controlled experiment from research into the vagaries of the weather.[1] The difference between controlled experiment and uncontrolled observation is, in fact, one of degree.

Observation that 'depends upon a definite interest and involves selection from the whole that is presented in experience is always of the nature of experiment, assuming that by an experiment is meant a controlled observation such that the number of variables is finite and known. The ideal of experiment is never attained. It would mean that the whole universe proceeded uniformly while

---

[1]Since it has been found possible to administer dry ice to hurricanes from aeroplanes, and thus artificially to induce rain, meteorology ought perhaps no longer to be classed among the sciences from which experiment is excluded.

we varied one ingredient.'[1] In practice we must recognise a scale from the almost wholly uncontrolled to the almost wholly controlled; but naturally, the degree of probability attaching to the results is likely to correspond to the position on this scale of the observations upon which these results are based.

The process of verification, it should be noticed, brings us back to the primitive test of sensory experience. The verification may, indeed, take the form of reading figures on a scale or making other measurements in a laboratory; but it is bound to demand the use of one of the five senses—generally the eyes. Scientific knowledge is thus based, at both ends, on the evidence of the senses. And '... there is one thing that is obvious from the start: only in so far as the initial perceptual datum is trustworthy can there be any reason for accepting the vast cosmic edifice of inference which is based upon it'.[2]

In the social sciences this final stage of the scientific process—empirical testing of the hypothesis—in its turn follows, in principle, the same course as in the natural sciences. Just as in the natural sciences this is the point at which controlled experiment is generally conclusive, so in the social sciences it is here that experimental methods are most seriously missed. But as has just been said, no hard and fast line separates controlled experiment from controlled observation. Hypothesis must be tested by the nearest approximation to controlled experiment that is available. And if this is conscientiously done, even in the social sciences hypotheses need no longer waste their fruitful potentialities in rank proliferation into the field of pure imagination.

In the absence of experiment, we must, however, normally be content with probabilities that fall in varying degrees short of certainty.

IV

Two further characteristics of scientific knowledge require notice. The first is its progressive character. It is of the essence of scientific

---

[1] Ritchie: *Scientific Method*, p. 21.
[2] *Human Knowledge* by Bertrand Russell (George Allen & Unwin), p. 22.

method that, by its use, additions to knowledge are cumulative through time. The researches of today illumine the dark places, improve the accuracy and extend the scope of the generalisations of yesterday. Some of the conclusions of earlier investigations are definitely proved wrong by later researches ; low probabilities are replaced by higher ones ; and year by year new additions are made to the body of knowledge. It follows that study of the work of scientists of an earlier generation is incidental to, rather than an integral part of, scientific learning. One may explore the history of, say, chemistry, because the lives of the great chemists, like those of other great men, have a human interest of their own ; or one may hope to learn from the study of the past something of the methods and conditions which are favourable to scientific progress ; or one may think that scientific discoveries which have stood the test of time are more clearly presented by those who first made them than in any later compilation ; or one may even find that the mistaken guesses of the past have a certain entertainment value of their own or are suggestive of other and more fruitful ideas in the present. But if one wishes to learn chemistry, it is the chemistry of today that is relevant with the latest discoveries included and the errors of the past excluded.

If the social sciences are scrupulous in their application of scientific method to such empirical data as lie in their peculiar province, they will inevitably become progressive in the way that the natural sciences are progressive. In some branches this is already beginning to be true. An out-of-date text book in psychology is frankly recognised as such, and in economics the physiocrats are not now taken very seriously. Progress may, however, be delayed by the persistence of a tradition which implicitly denies the claim of these studies to scientific rank. Certainly their place in academic curricula does not suggest that this claim is generally conceded, though their status is perhaps a little better in the United States than in Britain (and much worse in Germany than in either). The student of politics, for instance, must too often devote more attention to the reflections of Plato, Aristotle or Hobbes than to obscure monographs containing fresh additions to knowledge by modern research workers with admittedly no comparable claim to personal greatness. And he must do this not because (which would be a good reason) Plato, Aristotle or Hobbes were men of outstanding intellectual stature, contact with whose minds is a stimulating experience, but also because he is supposed to be as likely to find the right answers to his questions in their works as anywhere else. Contrast, for example, the part assigned to the works of Aristotle in a contemporary academic course on natural science and in one on politics. Obviously what Aristotle said on natural history can be safely ignored by the modern scientist (and without any implied diminution of his stature in his own time); but the student of politics does not show the same confidence that centuries have materially improved upon Aristotelian doctrines in that field. No doubt the difference may in part be due to the difference in the actual rate of progress of the scientific study of physical and political phenomena respectively; but we still appear to be reluctant to admit that, in so far as social research is fruitful, it *must* make obsolete the conclusions of even the greatest giants of earlier generations. Perhaps the need adequately to fill a curriculum has something to do with this. If the student of sociology did not have to wade through the biological monstrosities of Herbert Spencer, there might not be enough fully to occupy his time. We are, in fact, understandably shy of confessing that the amount of real knowledge is as small as it is; and we keep up the bluff by inflating our courses with the equivalent of pre-atomic physics and pre-Mendelian genetics. This might be passed off as a tedious, but fundamentally harmless, academic foible if it did not carry the dangerous implication that social studies are unprogressive and therefore unscientific.

The second peculiar characteristic of science is the predominantly quantitative nature of its conclusions. The associations discovered by scientific enquiry are not ordinarily of an all-or-nothing character: they are matters of more or less. The typical scientific law does not take the form 'if A then B': a more characteristic proposition would be 'if x degrees of A, then y degrees of B'. Indeed, the dependence of science upon measurement is a commonplace.

In order to see how far the measurements of social science are comparable with those of the natural sciences, it is necessary to call attention to one or two problems inherent in even some of the most familiar types of physical measurement. The simplest of all forms of measurement is, of course, the direct counting of physical objects, such as marbles in a bag or persons in a room. From this it is a small step to the use of standard weights and measures in order to measure such properties as length, weight or volume. In these cases we count not the actual properties to be measured, but the feet or inches on the yardstick, the ounces marked on the balance scale or the gradations inside the pint jug ; and here too the sensory check is not very far away. If anyone is indeed so sceptical as not to believe that a stick measuring two yards is twice as long as one measuring only one yard, he can convince himself by putting them side by side and measuring them directly against one another. To do this with two sacks of potatoes, one of which is alleged to be twice as heavy as the other, is rather more trouble ; but, if a balance is available, it can still, of course, be done by emptying the first sack till it just balances the second, and then similarly weighing in their turn the potatoes removed from the first sack against those left in the second. If instead of sacks of potatoes we had to deal with blocks of stone that we could not break, a direct check would not in practice be quite so easy ; but the fact that one can imagine doing with the stone what can actually be done with the potatoes gives confidence that the fundamental nature of the measurement is the same in both cases. By these somewhat cumbrous devices measurements of weight, length or volume can in the last resort be reduced to a process of direct counting which is subject to sensory check.

It is only necessary to mention such extremely elementary forms of measurement in order to call attention to their limited usefulness and to point the contrast with other forms of measurement also in common use. Consider, for example, the measurement of temperature. The sensation of heat is familiar to our senses; and most of us can distinguish between a cold bath, a tepid bath, a comfortably warm bath and a bath that is too hot to step into. We notice moreover that at certain extremes things happen to the water; when it is very cold it turns to ice; when it is very hot it boils. We are, however, quite unable to detect very fine degrees of difference, and there is nothing in the water that we can count. Indeed we cannot even accurately distinguish moderate differences in the temperature of our own bodies: if we could, hospitals would not need to be so careful to keep temperature charts out of sight of their patients. At this stage, however, the thermometer comes to the rescue, not merely distinguishing between the hot and the less hot, but actually grading differences on its scale, and so reducing the process of measurement to a matter of counting the degrees marked on the face of the thermometer.

This raises the question: how do we know that the measurements thus recorded are more than arbitrary conventions decided upon by the makers of thermometers? The matter is superficially complicated by the fact that the notation employed by thermometers in common use is clearly conventional in so far as the zero point in their scales is arbitrarily selected: what Centigrade chooses to call zero is 32 deg. to Fahrenheit. If, therefore, the Centigrade thermometer registers the temperature of one substance as 100 deg. and that of another as 50 deg., the corresponding figures on the Fahrenheit scale will be 212 deg. and 122 deg., i.e., by one reckoning the temperature of the first substance appears to be twice that of the second, whilst by the other the ratio is only 106/61. The apparent discrepancy is indeed explained by the difference in starting-point, but it illustrates the fact that these thermometers are measuring not absolute, but relative, temperatures. They merely tell you how any given temperature compares with that of melting ice.

More fundamental is the difficulty presented by the fact that while we can add one pound of potatoes to another pound of potatoes and get two pounds of potatoes, no corresponding operation can be performed upon temperatures. Two cups of tea each at a temperature of 50 deg. F. cannot be combined into one cup of tea at a temperature of 100 deg. F. On this account we can hardly be as confident about the validity of the statement that one room is twice as hot as another, as about the fact that one stick is twice as long as another. Indeed we may go as far as to describe the former as 'an assertion strictly without meaning'[1]; and there are those who would even argue that thermometer readings are wholly conventional—that temperature itself in fact is merely what a thermometer registers.[2]

Such a view is certainly repugnant to common sense, but it has to be mentioned here because, as appears below, a similar argument can be used—at first sight with more effectiveness—against the validity of some forms of measurement in the social sciences. It cannot perhaps be finally refuted, but there is another solid argument besides common sense that weighs against it : namely, that just as crude observation perceives certain associations between levels of temperature and other events (very hot water boils, very cold water turns to ice) so still other events are associated with the fine differences that the thermometer alone registers. All kinds of bodies expand and contract with variations in their temperature as recorded in the thermometer, and they do so with a consistency that is pleasing to science and powerfully supports the view that temperature is not just an invention of thermometers. And it is significant also that, as has been pointed out by J. W. N. Sullivan,[3] scientific men themselves continually seek to 'improve' the accuracy of their thermometers, regarding one instrument as 'better' than another if it is more effective in establishing reliable associations between phenomena ; whereas, if temperature was merely a reading upon a thermometer, there could be no reason for preferring any particular instrument to any other.

---

[1] *An Introduction to Logic and Scientific Method* by Morris R. Cohen and Ernest Nagel (Routledge), p. 294.
[2] For fuller discussion of this topic see J. W. N. Sullivan, *Limitations of Science* (Pelican Books), p. 209.
[3] *op cit.*, p. 210.

Finally, there are occasions when the measurement even of physical substances is not carried beyond the simple stage of placing the objects to be measured in a ranking order: quantitative intervals between them, such as the degrees on the thermometer, cannot be recorded. Measurement of the quality of hardness is a case in point. Empirical observation establishes what will scratch what: diamonds for instance will scratch glass. In this way a hierarchy of hardness, or 'scratching order', can be established; but we are still not able to take the further step of measuring how *much* harder one substance is than another. Measurement in the full sense is precluded because quantitative associations have not been established between the position of bodies in the scale of hardness and other physical events. Given such associations (as for instance those between temperature and the boiling points of various liquids) measurement becomes possible, even if only by indirect means: without them it is impossible.

V

The natural scientists do not need to trouble their heads overmuch about any problems as to the 'meaning' of the measurements which they make, many of which are, indeed, far more abstruse and abstract than the simple examples used here. They can go ahead cheerfully enough, measuring hypothetical entities that are never present to any of their five senses, and confident always in the sanction of an ultimate empirical check. If they map the unseen genes upon the chromosomes of cats, there is always the colour of the kittens to prove them right or wrong.

In the social sciences most measurements must be indirectly made, and few can be handled by any methods of counting. If of two events, one gives you a sensation of great, the other of only moderate, pleasure, you cannot lay your units of emotion end to end, and say that in the one case they would reach from here to New York, and in the other only to a point, to be thus determined, in mid-Atlantic. On this score, however, the social scientists can well take heart from the enormous rôle played by indirect measurement in the natural sciences; and, indeed, not only from that. For the problems of measurement in their world are not, I think, fundamentally different from those that occur in the measurement of natural phenomena. Just what those various problems are may be illustrated from four different types of social measurement now in more or less general use, namely: the measurement of intelligence; the measurement of public opinion; 'points systems' such as those used for establishing priorities in demobilisation from the Forces, or the right to a municipal house; and, finally, prices.

A common criticism of intelligence tests is that they measure only the ability to perform intelligence tests. This argument is, however, closely analogous to that which says that temperature is only a reading on a thermometer. For in the first instance we identify intelligence much as we identify heat—by crude inference from direct observation. We notice perhaps that people differ in the degree of success with which they manipulate their environment towards prescribed ends. We can classify those who are very successful, fairly successful or unsuccessful, as we distinguish between a hot and a tepid and a cold bath. The only material difference is that in the case of the bath water the perception is sensory and primary, whereas the abstract quality that we choose to label 'intelligence' is inferred from sense-observation of other people's behaviour: the behaviour alone, and not the intelligence, is accessible to the senses.

Again, as with the bath water, we are not always able confidently to distinguish fine differences, or even in all cases to be sure of the ranking order. But here, just as the thermometer came to the rescue in the measurement of the bath water, so does the intelligence test claim to solve the problem of measuring ability. And the intelligence test, like the thermometer, is subject to a continual process of 'improvement' designed to increase the accuracy of its measurements.

Suppose, for instance, that the intelligence of a group of English university students is tested by setting them a series of simple questions in Japanese. The great majority of—indeed probably all—the students would rank together at the zero level. Few would deny that the test would be 'improved' if it were translated into English. And from that admission we can proceed to argue, as many psychologists have, that still further 'improvement' would be effected if the tests were not purely verbal, but included exercises in the manipulation of non-verbal materials. Here again, as with the thermometer, the test of 'improvement' is the establishment of consistent associations with a group of factors other than the test itself, in a field which may indeed have only been vaguely defined. If the people who score high in an intelligence test comprise a larger proportion than does the population at large of men and women distinguished in scientific discovery or the arts or in chess-playing, or holding responsible positions in government and industry,[1] *something* is clearly measured beside mere skill in the performance of the test itself. The name to be given to that something is purely a matter of verbal convenience. In using the term 'intelligence' we have the advantage of keeping in harmony with established linguistic conventions. But whatever the name under which it passes, the measurement of that quality is an addition to scientific knowledge by virtue of the associations which it reveals : and a useful addition at that.

The intelligence test, like the thermometer, not merely ranges what it tests in a definite order, but professes also to measure the intervals between points on its scale. For this purpose, like the thermometer, it uses a conventional notation. The measurement of intelligence differs, however, from the measurement of temperature in that there is no convenient point of reference in the intelligence scale which serves as a counterpart to the freezing-point on the thermometer : intelligence does not melt, like ice, at a temperature of 32 deg. F. or 0 deg. C. Intelligence scales, therefore, must use a different kind of convention ; and they express their results, accordingly, not by reference to an arbitrarily chosen

---

[1] And they do. See, for example, *Psychological Approaches to the Biography of Genius* by Lewis M. Terman (Hamish Hamilton) especially pp. 13 ff.

point of departure, but in terms of a 'quotient' or relationship of the subject tested to the average level reached by a standard population, or by his percentile ranking in such a group.

This difference in notation does not, however, obscure the fundamental similarity that units of intelligence, like units of temperature, cannot, in any intelligible sense, be added together in the same way as pounds of cheese. Two intelligence quotients of 90 do not (alas !) add up to one I.Q. of 180. The parallel here between the recordings of the intelligence scale and readings on the thermometer is exact. The statement that one person is twice as intelligent as another has neither more nor less meaning than the statement that one room is twice as hot as another ; and the arguments for scepticism as to the possibility of making valid measurements of intelligence are likewise neither better nor worse than the arguments for scepticism as to the validity of measurements of temperature. And, of course, in either case the question of the potential measurability of the phenomena is unaffected by the degree of accuracy attained by any particular instrument that happens to be available. The fact that an ordinary thermometer may be a more refined and reliable instrument than any intelligence test yet devised is irrelevant to the question whether temperature on the one hand, or intelligence on the other, is susceptible of measurement.

Measurements of public opinion are of two kinds—those which merely seek to register the prevalence of specific opinions, and those which go further and interest themselves in the intensity with which given opinions are held. The problems that arise in connection with the former (or with surveys such as those which record the number of listeners to a particular wireless programme) are not really problems of measurement at all. For the difficulty in opinion surveys lies in identifying what it is you want to measure, not in the actual measuring of it. Thus in those surveys whose object is to forecast the voting in an election, the problem is to find a reliable index to the elector's future behaviour : people say, perhaps, that they will vote for one party, and in fact they vote for another. Or again, in surveys which are interested only in opinion as opinion, and not as a guide to future action such as voting, the problem is to devise a method of enquiry or to frame questions in a form which will elicit what people really think, and not what they think that they ought to think or think that the questioner wants them to think. A great deal of work has gone into improving the techniques of opinion polls in these respects, and the literature of the subject, particularly in the U.S.A., is abundant : but this is not due to problems of measurement. For when we have once chosen the index to be used, and we are ready to begin measurement, this proves to be the simplest of tasks : all we have to do is to count the people thus defined as holding one or other opinion.

Opinion polls and other surveys may, of course, go wrong through defective sampling : for one reason or another the people whose opinions have been recorded may not be representative of the whole population to be covered. Sampling, however, is a statistical technique common to many sciences. If it is improperly applied in the social sciences, the fault lies not in the nature of those sciences, but in the fact that they have employed bad technical methods : the remedy is simple—to use better ones. The only cases in which real difficulty occurs are those in which the publication of the result of a sample survey may itself affect the behaviour of the larger population : the sample, so to speak, makes itself unrepresentative. This is perhaps a special problem in election forecasts, where voting at the actual polls may be influenced by the known results of previous surveys. It has been suggested, for instance, that the pollsters' confidence that Mr. Dewey would win the 1948 presidential election in the United States acted as a last-minute goad to the supporters of Mr. Truman. But this factor is less likely to affect sample surveys other than those concerned with electoral opinion ; and notwithstanding these special difficulties the records of competently administered election surveys remain astonishingly good. Even in the Presidential election just mentioned, which is one of the few cases of substantial error, the Gallup Poll only gave Truman 5.5 per cent. less and Dewey 3.7 per cent.[1] more of the total votes than they respectively received. If this small percentage had not happened to turn the scale in the result of the election, little would have been heard of the miscalculation.

Estimates of the *intensity* of opinion, on the other hand, are genuine problems in indirect measurement. A crude device that may be used for this purpose is to present the persons whose opinions are to be measured with some alternative statements, asking each to indicate which of these most nearly expresses the strength of his own feeling. Suppose, for instance, that we wished to test the intensity of feeling amongst supporters of the government in power. Subjects might be asked which of the two following statements they would prefer to endorse: 'On the whole, I think this government's successes outweigh its failures': or 'I regard this government's achievements as simply marvellous'. Almost certainly, however, some would protest at such a narrow choice, and would want opportunity to express an intermediate opinion. In other words we should once more feel the urge to 'improve' the accuracy of the test, with the implication, as in the case of the thermometer and the intelligence test, that we are able to judge what 'improvement' is.

In opinion-measurement one method of effecting such improvement is to draw up a whole series of expressions of approval or disapproval of the Government of varying degrees of warmth. These are then submitted to a number of judges who range them in order of intensity. The persons whose opinions are to be tested are next presented with the series thus arranged and, as before, asked to indicate what entry in it is most conformable to their own feelings. The final result then appears in the form that x per cent. of the persons examined held the opinion with the degree of intensity conveyed in statement one, y per cent. with the lesser degree implied in statement two, and so on.[2]

---

[1] *Polls and Prophecies* by Henry Durant, *The Nineteenth Century*, December, 1948.
[2] For a study of more complex methods, see Hadley Cantril, *Gauging Public Opinion* (Princeton University Press), especially Chapter III.

This kind of measurement, however, still differs from that of the intelligence test (or the thermometer) in that, while it establishes an order of intensity, it makes no claim to measure the intervals in the scale. It does not even attempt to suggest that people who endorse the top statement in the series are eight degrees or five degrees or twenty degrees more passionate supporters of the government than those who choose the formula at the bottom of the list. Any such estimate would clearly be acknowledged to be 'arbitrary' in the sense in which the statement that your house is ten degrees but not fifteen or twenty degrees hotter than mine would not be so considered. But, as we have already seen in the case of the measurement of hardness, there are cases in which the measurements of physical qualities do not get beyond this stage. And in both natural and social science the reason is the same—namely, that consistent associations have not been established between the quantity to be measured and anything else.

The type of measurement which is attempted by various 'points' systems again has peculiarities of its own. In the execution of all such schemes three stages are necessary : the first is to select the factors by which the priorities in question are to be governed ; the second is to assign quantitative weights to each of these factors ; and the third is to ascertain in what degree each factor is present in any particular case. This last process is often simple enough and may well involve nothing beyond direct counting : thus, provided that the facts are available, the number of children of an applicant for a house, or the number of years that a soldier has served abroad, can be simply counted. On the other hand, in some cases where methods of this kind are employed, more difficult measurements may have to be made. In selecting candidates for promotion, for example, we may wish to estimate such specific qualities as intellectual ability, power of leadership or enthusiasm for the job, and we have few reliable means of testing any of these except, perhaps, intellectual ability. In principle, however, the difficulties encountered here are not different from those already discussed in connection with intelligence tests. The qualities to be measured are demonstrated in objective behaviour; and the only problem (though in practice it may be a large one) is to find a reliable method of recording variations in that behaviour.

It is more pertinent to ask what exactly is the status of the measurement which assigns weight to the various factors that enter into this type of calculation. From one point of view, the local authority's decision to give x points for size of family, y points for service in the armed forces, plus z points for being bombed out may be regarded as entirely subjective value-judgments. Different authorities will, in fact, use different ratings. And from this it might be concluded that such measurements are completely arbitrary and must be treated as fundamentally different from those already discussed.

From another angle, however, this is not so. Even these apparently arbitrary measurements are directed towards measuring factual data of the private psychological kind. They are in effect recordings of the state of mind of those who make them; and as such they are closely analogous to the measurements of opinion already discussed—the only difference being that in opinion-measurements the observer usually seeks to register the opinions of other people, whereas in these cases his object is to measure his own. Both make a contribution, even if only a small one, towards exact knowledge.

Finally, we come to the remarkable if familiar system of measurement contained in the prices at which goods and services are sold or offered for sale. It is perhaps worth pausing a moment to reflect on the fact that in the modern industrial world practically every object of human desire and practically every type of human effort is, or can be, priced; and that at every turn our actions and our way of life are regulated by these measurements—right from infancy, when a child learns to recognise that some things are unattainable because they are 'too dear', until the moment when the undertaker quotes one price for a grave in the front row and another for a less eligible situation. In this area of social life the habit of accepting precise measurements for the practical purposes of daily life is, indeed, quite astonishingly widespread and well established.

On the face of it, the price of an article measures the willingness of sellers to exchange it for money—that is to say for a claim on any other thing; and when sales take place, it simultaneously measures also the willingness of the buying public to part with such claims in exchange for the article in question. 'Willingness' in this context is of course a word which must be interpreted within the framework of whatever statutory regulations may be in force. A seller may be most anxious to charge more than the legally permitted price, and there may be plenty of buyers willing also to pay more; but the law forbids such a bargain. Still, we can at least say that people do not normally offer goods for sale except at prices which they are willing to accept: and equally that people do not buy things at prices which they are not willing to pay.

A market price is, therefore, rather like a thermometer hanging where it can be blown upon by streams of hot or cold air either from the right or from the left. If the buyer on one side blows hot, the price will rise: if there is a cold draught from the other side because sellers are glutted with stock, it will fall. When a sale takes place and the thermometer, as has just been said, *simultaneously* measures the willingness of the seller to sell and of the buyer to buy, it must, of course, follow that these two magnitudes are at that moment equal. In other words, both buyer and seller agree (for whatever reasons) to place the same valuation, in terms of all other saleable commodities, upon the article which is the subject of the transaction.

More than this we are not entitled to say. A system of measurement of this kind is, however, an extremely *convenient* (the choice of adjective is significant) instrument for a number of important purposes. It provides, for instance, a solution to a most intricate series of problems which faces all communities in which elaborate division of labour is practised and ambitious standards of living are aimed at—in particular, to the problems of distributing articles of which there cannot be an inexhaustible supply amongst all possible claimants, and of deciding what should be the priorities in production or in imports. The convenience of the system is at once obvious when we consider the alternative to it. If these questions are not decided by the movements of prices, they must be treated as matters of general policy. They are, however, essentially quantitative problems, and the conversion of general judgments into quantitative terms without the aid of any precisely marked yardstick is notoriously difficult. Any Englishman who has applied to the regional petroleum controller for a supplementary ration of motor fuel is well enough aware of the objections to regulating distribution otherwise than by prices—particularly perhaps, if he has opportunity of comparing the reply that he himself has received with those addressed to other applicants; and any manufacturer making articles that are subject to licence is equally well-informed—and often ready enough to be eloquent upon the subject.

The *convenience* of using a system of prices to settle these fundamental problems, therefore, creates a strong temptation to read into these measurements an interpretation which they will not bear: to argue, in short, that whoever is willing to pay the highest price for an article has also the best claim to have it; and that the things that are most profitable to produce are also those which ought to have priority in production. Particularly in a world where wealth is unequally distributed, this argument is, of course, quite indefensible. The difference between the woman who resolutely passes the shop window and the one who goes in and buys *may* lie in the intensity of their respective desires; but it is very likely to be a matter of the depth of their respective pockets.

We are thus faced in practice with a rather difficult choice: we can use a measuring-rod which has great attractions by way of convenience, but clearly does not tell us just what we really need to know. Alternatively, we can worry along without the help of any exact scale by which to determine priorities in production and distribution, in the belief that we shall get nearer the mark in this way than by using a measure which we cannot trust, and that the advantage thus gained is worth the inherent clumsiness and the incidental misjudgments of regulation by 'controls'. It seems clear that at the moment this choice must be made differently in different cases. We cannot risk leaving the satisfaction of our basic needs to settle itself in accordance with the movement of market prices; whereas, in the case of more luxurious articles, consideration of convenience may well turn the scale.

Some economists believe that this dilemma is not necessarily permanent; and that we might hope in time to construct a system of prices which would in fact measure the true urgency of consumers' needs and wishes as experienced by those consumers themselves; but that is too technical a matter to be discussed here. Pending the success of any plan of this kind, however, what we must not do is to misconstrue the meaning of existing prices, by pretending that they measure social valuations which are in fact quite outside their range; for that is like persuading yourself that you have had a square meal by falsifying the balance on which you have weighed inadequate ingredients.

The fact that increasing use is now made of various kinds of measurement in social affairs is an encouraging sign. It marks one of the first beginnings of really serious effort to treat social problems with the scientific accuracy and detachment that have long been recognised as essential for the understanding of material phenomena; and it has, moreover, considerable practical merits. It is, for instance, most beneficial for governments in democratic countries to be informed by precise surveys about the public's attitude towards their members and their policies, instead of deriving their view of this from their own, sometimes rather highly coloured, imaginations. And the one instance in which the use of an exact measuring-rod in social affairs seems to be declining—the case of the price mechanism—really points in the same direction; for its diminished use is merely the direct consequence of better appreciation of what it does, and what it does not, measure.

The growing practical use of methods of social measurement, moreover, confirms the belief that problems of measurement in social affairs are not inherently different from those with which the natural sciences are concerned. In both social and natural science there are quantities the measurement of which is demonstrably reliable; and others which we are not yet able to measure at all. It is, indeed, true that the measurements of the social sciences are more limited in scope, and cruder in technique, than those made by the natural scientists; but it is also true that the social scientists have not been on the job very long.

VI

I have given considerable emphasis to the problems of measurement in the social sciences, because of the recognised dependence of scientific progress in every field upon quantitative techniques. Attempts have sometimes, indeed, been made to prove that this dependence is more limited in the social than in the natural sciences—that in social investigation quantitative and qualitative techniques enjoy co-equal sovereignty over different parts of the territory, neither having precedence over the other. Thus Mr. Tom Harrisson speaks of 'the statistical obsession'[1] of the social sciences, and argues that the value of quantitative methods has been over-emphasised, making fun of the Clapham Committee on *Provision for Social and Economic Research* for their opinion that the more realistic and practical social research becomes, the more it requires computers, sorters, investigators and calculating machines. In Mr. Harrisson's view, sociological research demands 'an adequate admixture of words and numbers, of penetration and tabulation, representation and interpretation, understood situations and unimpeachable correlations, the raw material of life with the authentic statistic of validity'.

It is, indeed, true that much of the results of social research is still presented in descriptive, rather than in quantitative, form; but that is, none the less, the mark of the early stages of growth of a new science. Classification and description, as in biology, normally precede the power to reach quantitative conclusions; but they definitely represent a more primitive level of achieve-

[1] *What is Sociology?* by Tom Harrisson, *Pilot Papers*, March, 1947.

ment, if only for the reason that the significance of a qualitative conclusion cannot be assessed unless we have some means of judging how far it may be treated as typical. When Mr. Harrisson pleads the value of interviewing without formal questionnaires, or of the study of case histories or overheard conversations, as sociological tools *alternative* to quantitative methods, he overlooks the fact that the value of the results obtained by these methods entirely depends upon their quantitative significance. If you are trying to form a judgment of social attitudes by an 'extended close-up' study of one person, the results must be differently estimated according to whether your subject is a psychopath or a steady-going suburban paterfamilias; or if you go, as Mr. Harrisson suggests, to live amongst Grimsby fishermen in order to understand their way of life at first hand, you must certainly take pains to get to know not one or two, but a substantial *and representative* sample of the local people; and even then, the scope of your conclusions will be determined by how far Grimsby is itself a representative fishing town. The social sciences are not at all the victims of a 'quantitative obsession'. Like other branches of science, they cannot advance beyond quite elementary stages of development without the use of quantitative instruments.

Finally, we may remind ourselves that in the manipulation of quantitative data the methods of both social and natural science are identical. The statistical methods which are employed in physical or biological research are indistinguishable from those of the psychologist, economist or criminologist: correlations are established and variance is analysed by the same methods (and the significance of the results is the same) whether the figures involved relate to the incidence of cancer amongst mice or to socialist opinions amongst the professional classes. The increasing use of statistical techniques in many branches of scientific research has been a notable feature of recent developments. Here at least is common ground, on which both social and natural scientists can meet, speaking each other's language, perhaps occasionally sampling each other's jobs; and, we may hope, also fostering mutual understanding and respect.

CHAPTER THREE

PRE-SCIENTIFIC MENTAL HABITS

I

ALL scientific research depends for its fruitfulness upon an interaction between the work of the professional student and the attitudes of the public at large. The professional student must be faithful to the discipline of science and vigorous in his application of scientific method ; but he is not likely to get very far, nor are his numbers likely to multiply, in a social environment which is sceptical of his usefulness, if not actually hostile to him. Nor again in such conditions will much practical use be made of his discoveries. Moreover, the direction of scientific enquiry, even in countries where science is relatively free from direct political control, is inevitably conditioned in some degree by the focus of interest of the society in which the scientist lives. The preoccupation of the contemporary world with technical warfare has, for example, greatly stimulated the particular lines of research likely to be useful for this purpose ; though any one-sided development due to this particular cause may well prove to be only temporary, since the technique of warfare, which already involves physics, chemistry, meteorology, not to mention bacteriology, is likely to become still more comprehensive.

The relationship between the scientist and his social environment works both ways. On the one hand, he will languish in an indifferent or hostile world. On the other hand, hostility and scepticism will dissolve before convincing results. Scientific research above all things is judged by its fruits. When your diabetic symptoms yield to insulin treatment, when you recognise your wife on the television screen, or, better still, when you can destroy more people at one blow than have ever been simultaneously destroyed before, you appreciate the validity and the potentialities of the scientific method. The scientist's prestige rests ultimately on his ability to deliver the goods—particularly, today, the goods of military value.

If this is true of the natural scientist, it has even greater force for the worker in the social sciences. The requirements of scientific technique are, as has been emphasised in the preceding chapter, essentially the same in both fields, and must be satisfied with equal conscientiousness. But the social scientist, unlike his colleagues in physical or chemical research, cannot shut himself in an ivory laboratory. He is dependent on the co-operation of the public for his data; he is no less dependent on such co-operation for controlled observations by which to test his hypotheses; and, above all, he cannot deliver the goods to a public which neither knows, nor wishes to learn, how to use them, whilst too often he is powerless to demonstrate their usefulness himself. The criminologist, for instance, is not only at the mercy of the courts and penal institutions (and the criminals themselves) for the supply of his material and for opportunity to check his observations: his results must remain secret unless he can find a court willing to act upon them; whereas the engineer can at least build and operate a demonstration model. The relationship between the scientist and society is thus never so reliable or so agreeably circular in the social, as in the natural, sciences. The more we believe in the natural scientist, the more fruitful is his work: and the more fruitful his work, the more confident is our belief. In the social sciences this virtuous circle is liable to break in half.

The social sciences are, therefore, peculiarly dependent on recognition by the public at large (including of course statesmen and others upon whom rests the responsibility for actual decisions) of the possibility of a scientific approach to human problems. Such recognition is, however, far from being well established. On the contrary, pre-scientific mental habits are widely prevalent, and the canons of good empirical reasoning are seldom respected in the everyday discussion of public affairs. Carelessness in the use of data seems to be sadly widespread. To collect evidence of this, it is only necessary to note over a period of a week or two the generalisations made in ordinary conversation, the sole evidence for which is second- or third-hand hearsay : or the statements confidently introduced by the formula 'they say' which rest on the unchallenged authority of an unknown, and often unidentifiable, 'they' : not to mention the frank pieces of invention. Indeed, the scientific exploration of unscientific habits of thought on topics of public interest is itself a fruitful field for research, in which some pioneering work is already in progress.[1]

Particularly noticeable are the distortions that arise from disregard of the quantitative nature of most social data. Ninety per cent. (or alternatively ninety-nine per cent.) is a well-established synonym for 'a large proportion'. Questions which (like nearly all the significant issues in life) cannot but be matters of more or less are constantly answered in terms of yes or no, all or nothing.[2] Everything must be black or white : intermediate shades are ignored. If an institution is defective in some particular, it must be condemned outright. If a statute involves some irritating regulations, that is sufficient to damn it : little attempt is made to see these (often justly) annoying incidentals in the perspective of the major purpose which the law or institution is intended to serve.

Perhaps most widespread of all is the practice of ignoring the elementary principles of sampling, in terms of which alone valid generalisations can be made from selected members of a large population. Among the grosser deficiencies of this kind must be reckoned generalisations about the behaviour, opinions or conditions of foreign peoples based on the casual contacts of a tourist, or of a business man acquainted only with other business men in his own line ; or the similar generalisations which one social class likes to make about another. Less conspicuously distorted, but

---

[1] See, for instance, *A Study of a Rumour* by Festinger, Cartwright and others, *Human Relations*, Vol. 1, No. 4.
[2] This is especially true in politics : see below pp. 58ff.

hardly less misleading, are the generalised conclusions about human behaviour which are derived from relatively careful observation of a particular group, e.g., sailors, or academic persons, without regard to the factors which bias the recruitment of those groups or the specialised influences to which they are subject. The selection of sailors, for example, may be weighted by imperfect adaptation to certain aspects of settled life; and academic persons are almost certainly unrepresentative of the population at large on account of the high valuation which they set upon economic security and (we hope) on account also of superior intellectual ability. The professional student of the social sciences acquires an almost automatic habit of looking out for, and as far as possible discounting, bias in any sample; but he cannot but be struck by the unfamiliarity of this procedure even to many highly educated persons, including some whose technique for handling similar situations in the natural sciences would be rigorous in the extreme. Even on occasions when higher standards than those of casual conversation might be anticipated, there is still surprisingly little awareness of the need for scientifically designed procedures to estimate bias in, say, enquiries into public opinion. Although this is a field in which a great deal of attention has been paid to the technical problems[1] involved, there are still public and political bodies which ignore the dangers inherent in leading questions, or in inferences from questionnaires which are completed and posted by the recipient himself, with the consequent elimination of all evidence from those who are too apathetic or too hostile (or insufficiently hostile) to take this action.

Careless observation and slovenly handling of the data of social affairs are perhaps the most widespread of our pre-scientific mental habits, and the ones which seem to be least often discarded under the discipline of education. In other cases observations which themselves may be perfectly accurate are used as the foundation of fantastic hypotheses which, in turn, are treated as established laws of association without reference back to empirical

---

[1] See, for instance, any issue of the *Public Opinion Quarterly*.

data. Astrology affords a most conspicuous example. The data of the astrologer consist, on the one hand, of observed movements of the heavenly bodies and, on the other hand, of information supplied by his clients as to the dates of their births or other important events in their lives. Both sets of data are generally recorded quite correctly. The necessary astronomical observations are well established, and those who consult astrologers are as a rule accurately informed about their own birthdays. But the inferences drawn as to temperament and fate are completely ludicrous and never subjected to impartial empirical check. Yet astrological publications enjoy, apparently, an enormous sale.

I have already remarked upon the handicap imposed on the social sciences by their lack of technical terms. This handicap can, indeed, be overcome, though only by the establishment of a recognised technical vocabulary—a method unlikely to be adopted by any but highly-trained students. Linguistic confusion is, however, the cause of more serious trouble than mere inconvenience to the conscientious enquirer. In particular, in the absence of a clear nomenclature, it is fatally easy for discussions about things to degenerate, unperceived, into discussions about words. It is, indeed, no accident that the answer to so many popular questions must be prefaced with the formula 'it depends on what you mean by . . .' ; for until the issue of meaning is settled, discussion will almost inevitably be purely verbal and sterile. Consider, for example, such a question as whether, prior to the establishment of the State of Israel, the Jews were a nation. Without an accepted definition of the word 'nation' this is an entirely verbal issue. To say that the Jews were a nation because they had a common culture and believed themselves to be a nation, or, contrariwise, to refute this by the assertion that they could not have been a nation, because a nation is a community occupying a particular geographical area, is to engage in a purely linguistic controversy. The only matters of fact with which such a controversy can be concerned are the actual usages of the term 'nation' in common speech ; and these could be ascertained by statistical observation of current practice.

Since the word 'nation' has no divinely ordained, or inherent, meaning other than that which we choose to assign to it, a decision about this meaning is necessary before we can make an intelligible enquiry as to what groups may appropriately be described by that word. When, and only when, this decision has been reached (possibly after an investigation of prevailing verbal usage), is it possible to make classifications that add to our knowledge of non-verbal phenomena by distinguishing groups that are nations from those that are not.

Failure even by the participants to recognise the distinction between verbal and non-verbal issues is responsible for much sterile argumentation about social affairs. And this in turn is further aggravated by the strong emotional associations attached to particular words which often inhibit acceptance of precise definitions. The stultification that results may be illustrated from a common form of comparison between contemporary economic and social systems. This is clearly a subject of great practical importance, and one which would well repay accurate empirical investigation; but its exploration is constantly frustrated by the degeneration of a supposedly non-verbal into a purely verbal argument—and a highly emotional one at that. Which of us, for example, has not heard arguments about the relative merits of socialism and capitalism which proceed much as follows? One party contends that in a socialist society citizens are paid according to their needs, and not on the basis of the commercial value of their work. On the other side, it is pointed out that in Russia this is not in fact the method of payment adopted: on the contrary, there are great differences in earnings which are apparently related to differences in the demand for, and supply of, different types of skill. This in turn is met by a flat denial of Russia's claim to rank as a socialist society: the Russian system is to be classed as state capitalism, not socialism. At this point deadlock is reached, each party accusing the other of 'not knowing what socialism is'. The discussion has, in fact, degenerated into a sterile verbal issue. The question whether Russia is or is not a socialist country is a matter of linguistic convenience which should be settled in a moment by an agreed convention ; and inasmuch as the word 'socialism' has no precise technical meaning like that attached to the term *primula vulgaris*, it is a matter of indifference which way the matter is decided. Once this issue is settled, there are two possible non-verbal topics on which discussion can fruitfully take place. The first relates to the actual method of economic organisation in the U.S.S.R. : the second is the more general question of the merits, or the practicability, of alternative systems of distributing the national income. Argument about either (the former particularly) would of course still be futile unless supported by adequate empirical evidence.

The sterile discussions in which verbal issues are not distinguished from those that are non-verbal, or in which the various participants ascribe different meanings to the same word, naturally occur most frequently where strong emotional associations as for instance those attaching to the word 'socialism', are involved. Socialism to the socialist is something which must be kept pure and undefiled and free from taint of criticism : it is in fact often implicitly defined by him as the kind of social and economic system of which he approves—a definition hardly likely to commend itself to a professional anti-socialist. The futility of such discussions is, perhaps, best illustrated by reference to strictly analogous cases in which no such feelings are involved, and in which agreed definitions would immediately be adopted once the damage due to their absence was recognised. Imagine, for instance, a discussion about keeping fowls in which one party asserts that the difficulties of getting poultry-food, the restrictions on the disposal of eggs and the trouble of feeding the birds make poultry-keeping really more trouble than it is worth, at least as long as any controls are in force. To that the other party retorts that the birds practically look after themselves, special food is unnecessary and he experiences no red tape in disposing of his eggs. In due course it appears that the one speaker has in mind hens, the other is referring to geese : the discussion has been befogged by a confusion exactly parallel to that on which the socialist-capitalist argument broke down. At this point, if the parallel of that argument were followed, there would be a furious dispute on the question whether or not geese are 'poultry' or 'fowls'. In practice, of course, the stupidity of such a procedure would immediately be apparent, and further discussion would turn on the respective merits of geese and hens, each party having a perfectly clear and identical view of the birds to which these respective terms were understood to relate.

II

The general acceptance of scientific explanation of natural phenomena was not easily achieved. It was a slow business, accomplished in the face of opposition and, indeed, often of severe persecution. Such resistance is natural enough, since social institutions and customary modes of thought and behaviour tend to be adapted to the conditions of the past, not to those of the future. Even in the most revolutionary society, new knowledge is always uncomfortable: Dr. Darlington has, indeed, argued that, accustomed though we are today to the rapid strides of science, even contemporary academic institutions which are ostensibly centres of research are still strongly resistant to new discoveries in the natural sciences.[1] It is, therefore, no ground for surprise that a number of institutions in contemporary society tend to foster pre-scientific attitudes towards social phenomena.

The traditional categories of our educational system have some responsibility here. Particularly regrettable is the rigid division between arts and sciences. Since scientific method, as outlined in Chapter II of this book, is the only generally accepted method of advancing our knowledge of anything,[2] the restriction of the title 'science' to a particular part of the subject matter of education and research either involves the use of that term in a very awkward sense, or (and this, I think, is the more probable, though not

[1] *The Conflict of Science and Society* by C. D. Darlington, F.R.S. (Watts), p. 18.

[2] For a discussion of the claims of non-scientific sources of knowledge, see Chapter V.

explicitly recognised, alternative) carries the implication that the subjects known as 'arts' cannot be handled by scientific method, and in consequence that they are static and that our knowledge about them is not steadily progressive. This makes it the more unfortunate that social studies should find themselves, as they so often do, classified as arts and not as sciences. Certainly, whether or no classification of a field of study among arts is intended to imply that it is not susceptible of treatment by scientific method, it is in fact true that the empirical basis which is the foundation of all science is by no means firmly or universally established in 'non-scientific' subjects.

Insufficient emphasis on the empirical has further resulted, particularly in adult education, and in some university studies, in an altogether disproportionate emphasis on discussion, to the detriment of exact knowledge about the thing discussed. Discussion can be a valuable instrument of education in so far as it encourages the timid to overcome their shyness: it can be useful in promoting clarity of thought and expression: and, through the stimulus which one mind affords to another, it can be a fertile breeding ground for hypotheses. Such hypotheses cannot, however, add anything to knowledge unless they are first derived from adequate data, and subsequently checked back by reference to relevant facts. In my experience, contemporary education in subjects other than the natural sciences often definitely works *against* the development of scientific mental habits, because uninformed discussion is treated as equal, if not actually superior, to the acquisition of relevant information. Too often the student of the humanities 'discusses his problem' where the student of science 'learns his subject'.

Educational tradition is also perhaps responsible for another curious phenomenon which deserves notice in this context. Education in non-scientific subjects is largely concerned with the manipulation of verbal concepts. Clarity and conciseness of expression in speech or writing are certainly virtues, and ones which might with advantage be more assiduously cultivated by many students of the sciences. But a highly verbalistic type of education can result in the unjustified exaltation of excellence in expression as an end in itself, irrespective of what the words expressed may actually accomplish. Some of the most conspicuous examples are to be found in public life. Thus in commissions and conferences (particularly those which are international) a disproportionate amount of effort may be spent in the search for a form of words which all concerned can bring themselves to accept, even though they may hold widely divergent opinions; and the linguistic skill which is apt at devising such formulas commands a disproportionately high prestige. At times the effect of this process may be actually to obscure the arguments in favour of, or against, alternative courses of action. Yet the essential purpose of such conferences is to determine, or at least to advise upon, what should be done about the subject of their discussion.

Again, in Britain in the past century a profound change has come over the function of speech-making in the House of Commons. Before the tightening of party discipline which has accompanied the enlargement of the electorate since the middle of the nineteenth century, the purpose of making speeches in the House of Commons was to influence the votes of members, and thus to affect political action. Today, in the great majority of cases, members have made up their minds how they will vote before anybody opens his mouth on any subject in the Chamber; and in so far as their decisions are affected by listening to speeches at all, it is speeches in party meetings, and not those in the House, that count. Nevertheless, an enormous prestige attaches to a 'good speech' in the House. The zealous member will devote a great deal of care to its production; at least until he is well seasoned, he will suffer great apprehension at the ordeal of addressing so critical and knowledgeable an assembly; and if his performance is judged successful, he will be warmly congratulated by his fellow-members. In all this the standard of judgment is the quality of the speech in both form and content considered as an artistic performance, rather than any concrete practical result which it may have achieved. But the use of such a standard tends to invest Parliamentary speechifying with an altogether disproportionate importance, and to blind members of the House to a certain unreality which has crept into their proceedings. If it is salutary to weigh up the merits of a speech as a speech, it is equally salutary to consider in what way the world would have been different if it had never been made.

At the moment it may well be that parliamentary government with all its imperfections is the best means that we have been able to devise for combining tolerably efficient government with reasonable freedom for the governed. But I have little doubt that in the long run research in the social sciences will suggest much more satisfactory ways of achieving that combination than the (as they will eventually appear) crude instruments which we have so far evolved.[1] But in the meantime it is dangerous to allow complacency due to the use of false standards of judgment to obstruct the adaptation to changing conditions of the only instrument that we possess. I cannot but think that parliamentary procedure would be quickly and radically transformed if it was judged as a scientist judges efficiency for the purpose in view, rather than by standards derived from the excessive prestige enjoyed in our society by verbal achievement. And, moreover, in this scientific age, the under-representation in the House of men experienced in the methods of science is very remarkable.

In other ways also the structure of our social and political life both assumes and encourages pre-scientific mental habits. The assumption that two misrepresentations add up to one true representation is, for example, deep-seated in British law, politics and press. Perhaps it is an example of the sportsmanship for which the British are renowned. Certainly the 'attempt to reach the truth on any question by collating a number of partial and biased

---

[1] To avoid misunderstanding, it is perhaps desirable to say explicitly that this must not be construed as a hope that efficient dictatorship will supplant inefficient democracy. On the contrary, the hope is that social research will in time enable us to enjoy far more fully than we do at present the good things which we value in democracy.

accounts is a cumbrous and unsatisfactory procedure'.[1] In law there may be special reasons for the practice since the courts, both criminal and civil, normally deal with a conflict between two parties in circumstances in which it is vital that the interest of each should be fully safeguarded. Even in law, however, the inadequacy of efforts to reach the truth of admittedly technical matters from the conflicting evidence of experts is sometimes painfully clear; and the Continental system under which expert evidence is sought by the court and not by the contending parties has obvious advantages.

In politics the same principle underlies the two-party system of which the British, and in a less rigid form the Americans, are conspicuous champions. As a method of securing stable and tolerably consistent government, this system has much to commend it; and on that ground it is difficult to quarrel with the decision (which in effect commits us indefinitely to a two-party system) to rebuild the House of Commons with parallel benches arranged on each side of a gangway, instead of on the semicircular pattern favoured by many legislative assemblies elsewhere. Nevertheless, it cannot be said that a two-party political system, with its persistent implication that truth emerges from the clash of two errors, or, indeed, any party system at all as at present practised, is conducive to scientific habits of mind. In this respect, the price which we pay for stable government is high; and higher, I think, than it would be if we realised the cost more clearly.

In the first place, most of the significant issues in politics are matters of degree. To take an illustration from current political controversy, the Conservatives do not (mostly) propose to return the Post Office to private ownership: and the Labour Party has not suggested nationalising the performers who entertain theatre queues. There is no dispute about whether everything or nothing should be nationalised, but only about where the boundary line should be drawn. Should there be 10 per cent., 20 per cent. or

---

[1] Royal Commission on the Press, 1949, *Report*, para. 558.

50 per cent. more or less industry in public ownership ? Differences of degree, however, are not a good psychological basis on which to construct camps in violent opposition to one another. Hence for political purposes differences of degree have to be treated as differences of kind : the essentially quantitative and relative is translated into the qualitative and absolute—into categories, that is, which are generally incongruous with the results of scientific observation in any field.

Second, political controversies are a hopeless confusion of ends and means. There comes a point at which—as is suggested in Chapter VI—differences about ends cannot be resolved by any scientific process. In so far as political parties are divided by ultimate differences of this kind, the gulf between them is, indeed, as large as they like to make it out to be. Such divergences are, however, by definition unbridgeable by argument or evidence, so that *if* the parties are in fact separated by such differences of ultimate aim, much futile argumentation could be saved. *If* the Conservatives think that it is part of the hierarchical order prescribed by nature or by God that the lower classes should always be in a position of relative social and economic inferiority (though safeguarded against those extremes of insecurity or poverty which induce a sense of guilt in the secure and comfortable) ; and *if* members of the Labour Party seek complete and genuine equality, just because they like it that way, there is no more to be said. You pay your money and you take your choice.

In practice, however, it is not, at least on paper, at all clear what the ultimate aims of the parties are, and in particular whether they are the same, or different from one another. They fight one another furiously—ostensibly in pursuit of the same objectives : indeed, notwithstanding a fair knowledge of politics, I recently read half-way through the election address of a political candidate without discerning for which side he was standing. We are thus faced with an inescapable dilemma. Either the parties are substantially agreed on their vision of the New Jerusalem or they are not.

If they *are* so agreed, then the choice of roads to the common end in view is obviously a matter for exploration by scientific techniques, in which there is no reason to suppose that a Conservative will be superior to a member of the Labour Party, or *vice versa*. The prize will go to whichever makes the better hypothesis in the light of the better observation of data. And there is absolutely no reason why the exploration of roads to a common destination should not be undertaken jointly. Actually, of course, this seldom happens, except in some fields of foreign affairs, since political rivalry requires that each party should adhere to a distinct method of promoting the ends supposedly common to all. The citizen is expected to make his choice not in the light of evidence which could be, but seldom is, objectively examined, but on grounds of party sentiment. In politics we are so well used to this that it does not generally bother us much; but when the natural sciences are distorted by similar considerations, the intellectual monstrosity involved is immediately recognised. In the U.S.S.R. the Lysenko controversy has brought to light the fact that in that country the question whether or no you believe in the inheritance of acquired characters is a matter of political loyalty, not of inference from observation of plants and animals. Yet actually this is hardly more absurd than it is to treat the question whether nationalisation of industry promotes wealth, freedom and efficiency as a matter not of empirical observation but of political sentiment.

If, on the other hand, the parties are *not* headed for the same destination (which I think is nearer the truth), they should say so frankly. The elector could then vote for whichever goal appealed to him most; and naturally he would not, in that case, expect to see any party help any other in discovering the best route to a place to which it does not itself wish to travel.

As things are, however, we are driven to be partisans or cynics or both at once. When the programmes of all parties tend to resolve themselves into the same list of attractive generalities, we are driven to support, not the party whose policy appeals to us most, but the one which we believe to be most sincere in advocacy of the programme that is common to all. At the time of writing I have before me the addresses of Labour and Conservative candidates seeking election to local councils. Both are emphatic about the vigour with which, if elected, they will build houses and schools. If both equally mean what they say, there can be no reason why they should be fighting one another: if they differ only on the subject of the most efficient way of getting houses built, that is a question of method best explored by unprejudiced scientific enquiry—an enterprise in which again they could both wholeheartedly co-operate so long as they are agreed on the purpose which the enquiry is to serve. The fact that political parties show no sign of recognising the logic of this argument inevitably creates the suspicion that their real objectives are not quite so much alike as they are inclined to pretend when elections are near. That is what makes us cynics.

The dangers of this situation are, I think, insufficiently realised by the professional politicians. Yet cynicism is the most dangerous enemy of democratic forms of government. It must be a matter of conjecture, but I am inclined to think that in the British General Elections of 1945 and February, 1950, all parties underestimated (though not all in the same degree) the capacity of the public to detect insincerity, and to appreciate that conclusions must rest on factual evidence. If so, the remedy, even within the framework of party politics, is simple—more intellectual honesty in political propaganda. Certainly the present situation with its fictitious agreement about ends at election times, and its disagreement and partisan choice of means between-whiles, gives us the worst of both worlds. Small wonder if the elector writes off the whole field of public affairs as outside the domain of scientific enquiry.

That attitude is, in turn, reinforced by the press. The picture which most of us get of the world of affairs is mainly derived from the newspapers; and this is several degrees removed from that precise observation of data which is always the basis of scientific enquiry. In the first place, most newspapers are the spokesmen of one or other of the political parties. It is true that, according to evidence given before the Royal Commission on the Press,[1] news and opinion are supposed to be strictly separated; but the Royal Commission's own researches suggest[2] that this distinction is very imperfectly observed in practice. Certainly it does not generally require any close scrutiny of the news columns of a paper to detect where it stands politically.

Secondly, as the Commission also emphasised, the world as presented in the newspapers is further distorted by each particular paper's conception of the elusive quality known as news-value. The one essential ingredient necessary for an event to have 'news-value' for any paper seems to be that it should stand out as something unusual or exceptional. Given that peculiarity, a further criterion is applied by each paper in accordance with its own particular field of interest, some giving prominence to 'human interest', while others are interested only in publicising the words and doings of people already well known. Finally, the attitude of some sections of the press to the difference between fact and fiction would fill any scientific investigator with horror. A regular correspondent of the *Observer* blandly writes: '*Departing from journalistic practice*, I admit that I made a mistake'[3]; while according to Mr. Bernard Hall of the *Daily Express*[4] a fact for newspaper purposes is whatever an editor sincerely (even if mistakenly) believes to be a fact.

All this, as the Royal Commission's Report recognised, may well be the natural consequence of a newspaper's need to pay its way like any other commercial enterprise. It is not a question of assigning praise or blame to the press. What matters is the stark fact that 'the newspapers, with few exceptions, fail to supply the electorate with adequate materials for sound political judgment'.[5]

---

[1] Royal Commission on the Press, *Report*, para. 370.
[2] *Ibid.* Appendix VII.
[3] Pendennis in *The Observer*, 24th April, 1949. (Italics mine.)
[4] Royal Commission on the Press, *Minutes of Evidence*, Q.1459-76; and *Report*, para. 553.
[5] Royal Commission on the Press, *Report*, para. 572.

PRE-SCIENTIFIC MENTAL HABITS

The citizen who reads one paper only is, at best, presented with a view of the world which is doctored to suit the ideology (using that word in its widest sense) of that particular organ. He is daily nourished on a mental diet in which conclusion normally precedes evidence, and in which observation is directed to support, not to check, hypothesis. At worst, if he reads one of the more sensational and less scrupulous papers, he may even be led 'to forget that conclusions are, or should be, grounded upon evidence'.[1] And to protect himself against these perversions, he must resort, as we have seen, to the devious method of correcting the distortions of one paper by those of another. Nothing could be further from the methods of science.

III

Political parties carry labels; and each party commonly seeks to stimulate group feeling amongst its members and sympathisers by attaching favourable sentiments to its own label and opprobrious ones to those of its opponents. In addition, party colours, songs and similar devices are used to give added strength to these sentiments. From one point of view, these labels may be regarded as merely abbreviated descriptions of a bundle of practical proposals, policies and attitudes. In Britain in 1950 a Conservative is opposed to any further nationalisation of industry and generally lays emphasis (in the intervals between election campaigns) on the cost, rather than on the beneficial results, of the social services, particularly those that are of recent origin. People who describe themselves as 'Labour' have a number of industries still on the list for nationalisation, and emphasise what the social services are doing for the health and welfare of the people. Communists think that wages ought to be higher, the cost of living lower, and the social services more generous. Nearly all political labels are, however, more or less closely related to a wider philosophy. Conservatives do not like change, the Labour party is associated with

---

[1] Royal Commission on the Press, *Report*, para. 559.

socialism, Communists are all mixed up with the philosophies of Marx, and Liberal can be written with a small 'l' as well as a large one. These wider philosophies also have labels of their own, nearly all of which end in ' 'ism' : they are, in fact, more or less comprehensive intellectual systems, and, as such, belong to the much more extensive class of philosophical systems which use the same termination—idealism, materialism, logical positivism and so forth.

All these philosophies are dangerous on account of just this implicit claim to comprehensiveness. Most at least of the political 'isms have, no doubt, an empirical origin, even if this is now remote ; but when a body of generalisations takes to itself a title ending in 'ism, that is usually tantamount to proclaiming its divorce from further empirical investigation. It has become a *system* from which the answers to future practical problems are supposed to be derived by deduction without reference back to observed data. In time the empirical origin of these systems tends, indeed, to be so far forgotten that they are converted into virtual dogmas—first principles, accepted as a matter of faith ; and they may also, as has sometimes happened disastrously in the case of socialism, become just channels of escape from reality, or excuses for inattention to the data of experience. The socialist who refuses to form a judgment upon any immediate social problem because under a socialist system no such problem would arise has become a pathetically familiar figure[1]; though happily his influence has been greatly diminished since the responsibilities of actual government were thrust upon a professedly socialist party in 1945.

The tendency to think in terms of comprehensive and even dogmatic systems is in fundamental conflict with all scientific enquiry. It is significant that words ending in 'ism are lacking in the natural sciences. And their next of kin—words ending in 'ist —are used only to describe persons who have specialised knowledge of a particular field of natural science, not those who pay allegiance to a particular body of doctrine. A zoologist is a man

---

[1] For further discussion of this melancholy topic, see my article *A Plague on All Your 'isms* in the *Political Quarterly*, January-March, 1942.

who knows about living creatures, not one who holds particular theories about life. Because of the unfortunate associations which the 'ism termination has thus acquired it is, I think, regrettable that many of those who wish to emphasise their explicit rejection of dogmatic systems do so by coining a fresh 'ism word of their own : I have in mind particularly 'humanists' and 'humanism'.

Everything which encourages the habit of interpreting social phenomena in terms of preconceived systems obstructs the growth of a scientific approach to human affairs ; and such systems are not the bane only of political thinking. Even more significant is the place occupied by religious dogmas. The grounds on which religious doctrines rest their claim to validity are discussed more fully in Chapter V. Here it is relevant only to emphasise the enormous tracts of life throughout which their truth is simply taken for granted. In Britain, where there is still an established Church, the proceedings of the House of Commons are daily opened with prayers, and nearly all important public ceremonials include some form of religious observance. The Education Act of 1944 provided that in every publicly-aided school the day should begin with an act of religious worship[1]; and over and above the considerable period assigned for services on Sundays, religious talks or readings are broadcast daily over the air.

The volume of church attendances suggests that a good deal of this effort makes perhaps no very profound impression. Moreover, the sceptical parent may withdraw his child from religious instruction ; the blasphemy laws are not in fact invoked against writings that repudiate religious dogmas ; and from time to time a broadcast talk or discussion criticises assumptions which on every other day are implicitly accepted. Nevertheless, the cumulative effect of the repetition of dogmas should not be underestimated. Religious teachings cover many of the most important fields of human interest, including both man's place in the universe and the whole field of morals ; but whatever may be the way by which religious conclusions are reached, it is not the process of

---

[1] The Act omits to say worship of what.

scientific enquiry described in Chapter II of this book. From an early age, therefore, most of us find large tracts of experience reserved as the province not of science but of religion ; and the development of scientific habits of thought is correspondingly cramped and inhibited.

IV

Great then are the forces in education, politics, press and religion which are ranged on the side of pre-scientific mental attitudes towards human problems. These forces are, moreover, powerfully supported by quislings within the human mind itself. The problems of the social sciences differ from those of natural science, in that practically all dealings between human beings involve emotion ; and, unfortunately, we are not so constituted that the action most likely to promote a desired end is also always the action emotionally most satisfactory to the doer. Daily life abounds with examples of this. Most of us have observed conversations which, though ostensibly intended to entertain the listener, in fact only served the purpose of relieving the feelings of the speaker. The theory of punishment, again, rests largely upon the principle that, if the offender is made to suffer sufficiently, he will come to see the error of his ways. Yet actually there is little experience that supports, and much that contradicts, the view that people can be brought by force to see the error of their ways. Force may certainly induce them to change their behaviour for reasons of external convenience ; but that is quite another matter. It is, indeed, tragic to reflect how largely this fallacious doctrine still dominates current penal practice : or what enormous influence it enjoyed in the countries fighting against Germany in the two world wars of this century. Actually, of course, such theories are simply rationalisations of primitive impulses of revenge. 'I will kick you because I hate you for what you have done to me' is one argument ; 'I will kick you so that you are too frightened to do such a thing again' is another ; and 'I will kick you till you realise what a beast you are' is a third. The emotional attraction of the first of these threats leads us to confuse it not only with the second (with which, indeed, it may well be combined) but even with the third, with which it is in practice normally incompatible.

Formidable though these obstacles are, however, it must not be forgotten that the natural sciences have themselves had to fight comparable battles : to say nothing of the long record of actual persecution suffered by the pioneers of science. Resistance to all science, both natural and social, involves an element of self-esteem : science begins with somebody else's more careful observation of phenomena which we have less accurately observed for ourselves. Conquest of this resistance even by the natural sciences is not yet complete. In many parts of the world magical practices still offer formidable opposition to scientific medicine ; and the 'practical' farmer continues to back his own judgment, sometimes rightly because his observation is better, but often wrongly from prejudice, against the experts of the Ministry of Agriculture. Even those who are scientifically sophisticated still feel the urge, when faced with the breakdown of some mechanical contrivance, to wreak physical violence upon the offending (the adjective is significant) object : to kick the tyre that develops an ill-timed puncture, or to shake the clock that has stopped, with dangerous vehemence. Mostly we have learned to restrain this impulse in favour of more constructive measures ; and, if emotional release is imperative, to find it in verbal expletives which do not hinder, if they do not help, the solution of the problem. Yet often, adults will encourage in children follies which they have outgrown themselves, urging the child to beat and denounce the 'naughty stone' against which he has accidentally stumbled. But as with the natural sciences, so also with social science, nothing will succeed like success. Repeated demonstration to primary sensory or emotional experience of the correctness of scientifically established propositions wins in the end : seeing is believing, and repetition is not vain.

Nor must it be assumed that most of us are inherently incapable of the mental adjustments necessary if the potentialities of scientific method in human affairs are to be fully realised ; or that the invasion of this province by science would simply put an end to common conversation ; or even, finally, that a scientific approach to human problems would paralyse action. Nobody who has listened to spectators at a football match subsequently discussing the events of the game can doubt that extremely acute observation is quite a common faculty even amongst those who have had little formal education. In the law courts also, the ordinary citizen is required to conform to extremely high standards of accuracy. Our retention of the jury system is evidence that he is believed to be capable of what is required, though perhaps in this particular case optimism goes too far. Certainly, scientific methods of reasoning are widely practised in the fields in which they are understood to be appropriate. In discussions about the qualities of objects in daily use, such as radio sets or cars, observation (apart from some obvious boasting) is creditably accurate—certainly far above the standard expected in the discussion of human affairs. In these fields hearsay is usually accepted with reserve, until it has been subjected to empirical check. The remarkable improvement in the performance of X's car, said to be due to the use of a certain gadget, is met with the significant reply : 'well, I must *try it* on mine.' And anybody who held that the poor tone of his radio was explained by the fact that he bought it under the sign of Capricorn would be generally regarded as crazy. It is not superior ability that is required to apply these standards to human as well as to mechanical problems, but realisation of the fact that they would be in place there. Certainly the abundance of current discussion of the ingenious devices of our civilisation should lay to rest any fear that recognition of scientific technique must reduce the layman to silence. To extend that recognition to the territory of social affairs would, indeed, inhibit the visitor who returns from Germany prepared to answer questions on 'what the Germans' think ; but it would not prevent him from saying that the Germans whom he met were predominantly of such and such a class with such and such a background, and proceeding to quote the opinions which he heard with some indication of their relative frequency. The advantage of the latter form of statement over the former is that it is likely to be true.

As for action—in real life, action on insufficient knowledge is continually necessary. A sensible person is not paralysed by the obvious discovery that without sufficient knowledge he must make a rough calculation of probabilities. He does not refrain from applying for a post which he thinks on the whole would suit him, because he cannot be as sure of this as a bench of magistrates are supposed to be before they make a finding of guilt. His uncertainty merely makes him more anxious to get such additional data as he can.

Nor is it just repeating the errors of the nineteenth-century Utilitarians to suggest that a general growth of more scientific attitudes towards social problems is in no way inherently impossible. The theories of the Utilitarians were largely built upon the assumption that both in personal and in public affairs the ordinary man normally acted by scientific inference from relevant data. The pioneering observations of Graham Wallas[1] in politics, and the formidable explorations of contemporary psychologists into unconscious motives have made short work of that. People do not behave in the rational way that the Utilitarians lightheartedly assumed, nor, as I have tried to show in this chapter, is that how they are conditioned to behave by contemporary social institutions. This, however, is no ground for supposing that an appropriate modification of those institutions could not promote more rational attitudes and encourage the application to social problems of habits of thought which present no difficulty in other fields. The Utilitarians in effect postulated—and in this they were obviously right—that the problems of human life could only be effectively handled by the technique of rational thought, which is also the foundation of science. The further inference that these

---

[1] Especially in *Human Nature in Politics*. The discoveries of this book were quite startling when they first appeared: if they look commonplace now, that is the measure of its accuracy and wisdom.

problems would in fact be so handled under the nineteenth-century system of political democracy in the social, religious and educational environment of that time were quite fallacious ; but not more fallacious than the supposition that that is the end of the matter. The argument presented in this chapter may, indeed, be in the direct line of descent from Bentham and Mill : but it is not the work of their resurrected ghosts.

CHAPTER FOUR

TWO BLIND ALLEYS

I

THE application of scientific method in any field calls for standards of accuracy in observation, imagination in the framing of hypotheses, and care in checking these in turn against further observations—all at a level which is never easy to attain. In the sphere of social problems these virtues are, as has been emphasised in the preceding chapter, at a discount amongst the general public. Most of us never handle these problems even when they impinge upon ourselves with the same measure of scientific care as we should normally apply to any problem arising from the use of everyday mechanical objects, or in such hobbies as gardening or photography; nor do we ordinarily look for help from the professional workers who make it their business to study social questions in a scientific way.

This makes it exceptionally important that the exploration of these problems by professional students and by the makers of opinion should be scientifically accurate and fruitful. The social sciences are, indeed, still very young; and in the early stages of any science it is inevitable that there should be a good deal of aimless floundering, and that we should sometimes take the wrong turnings. This would not, indeed, matter very much, were it not for the fact that many blind alleys are long ones, and that we do not always recognise this till we have gone a very long way off the right track. Each successive enquirer is, moreover, very naturally inclined to follow the lines laid down by his predecessors and to think in the terms that they have made familiar: errors as well as discoveries can thus be cumulative. At the present stage the social scientist has, obviously, nearly everything still to learn ; but, unhappily, he has already something to forget.

The two main causes of confusion and sterility in sociological studies appear, up till now, to have been on the one hand muddled biological analogies : and, on the other hand, the influence of the pseudo-scientific system associated with the name of Marx. The first is due to a misconception of the nature of the data of social science : the second, which is discussed more fully in the second section of this chapter, is caused by failure to disencumber ourselves from pre-scientific mental swaddling clothes.

The essence of the muddled biological analogies is that they treat human 'societies' (not human beings) as organisms. The confusion is the more lamentable because human beings (but not human societies) are animal species, and the social sciences, as I shall suggest later, must therefore be grounded in biology. But the false parallel between 'society' and an organism appears to have an almost irresistible attraction. It occurs with disastrous persistence in the works of pseudo-scientific sociologists and historians—in Herbert Spencer's specious and detailed analogies ; in Oswald Spengler's theories of the life-cycle of civilisations ; in Arnold Toynbee's monumental attempt to provide a scientific explanation of the whole of human history ; as well as in the work of many less widely known authors. The basic hypothesis of all these theories is that the life of human societies or civilisations can be explained in terms such as birth, growth, maturity, decay and death, which are derived from the life-cycle of an organism ; and that this explanation is an empirically justifiable—that is to say a scientific—proposition, and not merely a picturesque metaphor. Indeed, Dr. Toynbee, who is the most powerful contemporary exponent of such an hypothesis, explicitly attacks Spengler on the ground that his method is to 'set up a metaphor and then proceed to argue from it as if it were a law based on observed phenomena.'[1]
Yet Toynbee is himself extremely detailed in his biological analo-

---

[1] *A Study of History* by Arnold J. Toynbee (Oxford University Press). Abridgement of Vols. I-VI by D. C. Somervell, p. 248.

gies, while claiming for his own work the status of an essay in the application of 'scientific technique' to human history.[1] Not only does he apply the terms birth, parental influence, maturity, procreation, arrested development and death to human societies or civilisations : he even goes so far as to trace genealogies of civilisations, relating them to one another as parent to child even down to the second and third generation.[2] Actually the chief difference between Spengler's and Toynbee's biological theories seems to be that whereas in Spengler's view every civilisation must eventually die, Toynbee finds no 'must' about it, although so far death has, in his view, overtaken most of them.

All these quasi-biological interpretations involve fundamental confusions of thought, and open the door to disastrous fallacies. Most deep-seated of all is the confusion between a human society, in the sense of *a number of human beings* having mutual relationships, and *the way of life* followed by the members of any such group—confusion, that is to say, between the physiological life-cycle of human beings and the ideological life-cycle of a culture-pattern. It is this muddle that is responsible, for example, for much nonsense about the 'death' of societies or civilisations. Physiological death obviously overtakes every human being within not more than about a hundred years from the date of his birth, so that the members of any group who are alive at a given date will all be dead a century or so later : it clearly cannot be this obvious fact which quasi-biological sociologists have in mind when they refer to the 'death' of a society. On the other hand, if a 'society' means any group of human beings who follow common ways of life, together with their descendants, in that sense death is extremely rare. A few local sub-varieties of our species, the pre-colonial inhabitants of some West Indian islands, for instance, have become virtually 'dead' in this sense. Such exceptions are, however, few and far between, and we may say that as a general rule human groups, especially if they are of any size, perpetuate themselves ;

[1] *Op. cit*, p. 47.
[2] *A Study of History* by Arnold J. Toynbee (Oxford University Press), Vol. I.

though they do not, of course, maintain the same numbers generation by generation, and they may lose their biological distinctness by intermarriage with other groups—as for instance the Mexicans did under Spanish rule.

Clearly, then, the death which overtakes societies or civilisations does not mean the physiological death of the persons of whom generation by generation those societies are composed, any more than what Toynbee calls an 'arrested' civilisation means one whose members failed to attain their full physical stature, owing to malnutrition or some such cause. The death of Hellenic civilisation does not mean that the classical Greeks left no descendants to ride today in buses in the land where Socrates once argued and Pericles practised statesmanship. It would, indeed, be superfluous to consider such a patently silly interpretation were it not that, as we shall see later, inferences are drawn from the life-cycle of societies which could only be valid if the physical death of their members was involved.

Discussions of the life-cycle and possible death of a society must, therefore, be intended to refer to the life-cycle not of human beings but of a way of life. The biological concepts of birth, growth and death are, however, here quite inapplicable: indeed, they are meaningless. Before one can describe the life-cycle of an organism and trace its genealogy, one must be able to identify it with precision, otherwise nobody, not excluding the scientist himself, knows what is being talked about. Dr. Toynbee does, indeed, try to satisfy this condition by making an actual count of human societies, living or dead. This count gives a total of twenty-one civilisations, of which fourteen are already dead; while two were 'abortive', and some half-dozen have been 'arrested'.[1] To these civilised societies we have to add about 650 'primitive' societies, counted in 1915, and an unknown but much larger number of primitives that are now extinct.

This precision, however, turns out to be quite illusory. According to Dr. Toynbee, a civilisation is to be defined as 'an intelligible

---

[1] *Study of History*, Abridgement, pp. 33, 34, 153, 164.

field of study'—a description which cannot but provoke the comment—intelligible to whom ? To that, however, there appears to be no answer, since the enumerator himself admits that he is uncertain whether the total of civilisations should be nineteen or twenty-one—the answer depending on whether the orthodox Christian society should count as one or two (Orthodox-Byzantine and Orthodox-Russian), and whether the Far Eastern should be similarly divided into Chinese and Korean-Japanese. Such vagueness about boundary lines would be of no account if the life-cycle theory was treated as no more than a metaphor ; nor would uncertainty as to the total number of societies necessarily be fatal to a scientific hypothesis, if it arose merely from insufficiency of records, with the consequent likelihood that some societies had been missed. For if there was reason to believe that the known specimens were sufficiently representative, a theory might properly be built upon them alone. But for the count to be doubtful *because no one knows exactly where one unit ends and another begins* makes nonsense of the whole business. It would be no less foolish to set about making a population census without being able to decide whether two people who happened to be standing close together at the time of the count, or who were near relations, should be reckoned as one or two units. If we cannot identify an organism sufficiently well to distinguish one of it from two of it, we are certainly in no position to make scientific generalisations about its life-cycle or to compare one specimen with another. For a father to live on with his habits perhaps changing during life is one thing : for him to die, and leave a son who has both inherited some of his father's genes and been influenced by his father's upbringing, is another. A geneticist (or indeed any sane person) who did not know the difference would look pretty ridiculous.

Whatever the claims made for them, descriptions of human societies in terms appropriate to biological organisms must, therefore, be regarded as metaphorical. In some respects, moreover, they are particularly insidious metaphors. Applied to any individual organism, such epithets as mature, arrested, decaying or dead, have an objective meaning: the difference between a fully-grown cow, a senile cow and a dead cow is a matter of established scientific observation, and not, unless in rare exceptional cases, subject to dispute. Civilisations, however, not being organisms, and the use of such descriptions being in their case necessarily metaphorical, no such objective meaning is available. What we can say is, of course, that civilisations *change*: that the prevailing ways of life are modified in course of time, and that they are different in different places. The whole complex of causes responsible for these changes is an important field of study for the social scientist, and one in which knowledge is still extremely patchy. If it does not take much insight to see that the adventures of Commander Perry had a good deal to do with the revolution in Japanese culture in the later nineteenth century, it is, nevertheless, not so clear why Frenchmen salute one another with a kiss, and the British regard the practice as unmanly. Marx notwithstanding, few general laws of association are yet established in this field.

Change, however, is one thing: birth, growth and death quite others. For what, after all, is the standard by which we distinguish the infancy, the prime, the old age and the death of any given civilisation, or by which we compare the degree of maturity reached by one with that attained by another? In common usage it would seem that the basic difference between 'primitive' (including 'arrested') and 'advanced' societies is generally reckoned in terms of the degree of elaboration of material technique. This criterion would, however, be horrifying to so whole-hearted an anti-materialist as Dr. Toynbee. Indeed, he expressly warns us against mistaking either technical skill or complexity of social institutions for a sign of advanced civilisation.[1] Yet, some of the societies whose development Dr. Toynbee stigmatises as 'arrested' appear to have had a serenity of outlook which one might have expected him to regard as a mark of great maturity. Alternatively, artistic or literary achievement may be used as the criterion of

---

[1] *Study of History*, Abridgement, p. 193.

growth : the maturity and the decay of Athenian civilisation are generally reckoned in these terms. But, in the first place, this involves the large assumption that the standards by which we judge the artistic performance of other peoples have an objectivity comparable to that of the standard by which we judge the physiological maturity or senescence of an organism[1] ; and secondly, this is not a criterion which we are generally prepared to use in practice at all consistently. It would involve, for instance, rating the Romans as arrested in comparison with the Greeks ; and it would stamp contemporary Americans firmly with the mark of immaturity.

Such valuations will, to be sure, find many supporters ; but that does not conceal the fact that they are quite subjective, and that they certainly have nothing to do with the physiological concepts of birth, growth and death. If anybody chooses to say that the Roman Republic, and the various ways of life that prevailed amongst the Romans in the time of the Republic, had a beginning, a middle period and an end, that is an accurate chronological observation—but obviously one not worth making. But when we proceed beyond that to describe the life of the Republic in terms such as are applicable only to true biological organisms, what really happens is that essentially subjective valuations slip into the picture without being explicitly stated. That is the danger. Terms derived from the life-cycle of an organism are not emotionally neutral when applied to human beings. Maturity sounds, in the ordinary case, a more desirable condition than a state of arrested development ; and to most of us the prospect of death or decay is unpleasing. The sociologist who labels a civilisation as decaying is in effect expressing the opinion that the people concerned in it have changed from a way of life that he admires to one which he finds less admirable : the term 'growing' implies an opposite movement—upward in the particular scale of values that the writer favours ; while 'arrested' means that a people have failed to make achievements of which he would have approved. We

---

[1] The implications of this are more fully discussed in Chapter VII.

need not deny that the measurement of civilisations by *explicitly stated* standards capable of reasonably precise definitions (e.g., technical skill or artistic achievement) may have its uses ; and no one would wish to exclude subjective judgments, provided always that the scale of values favoured by those who make them is stated as clearly as possible. What is scientifically objectionable is the theft of objective terms from biology to cover implicit, subjective value-judgments derived from standards that are not divulged.

The greater the length to which organic theories of society are carried, and the more precise the terms to which they are reduced, the more starkly is their unscientific and essentially metaphorical character betrayed. Since biological evolution is the result of natural selection, a parallel selective process is sometimes supposed to be responsible for social evolution. In actual fact, however, natural selection operates only through physical death : the organism which fails to adapt itself sufficiently to its environment comes to a physical end, and is no longer here to tell the tale. As we have already seen, death in this sense is not normally operative among human societies. The idea of natural selection between *civilisations* or ways of life is, therefore, meaningless. Within the limits set by the need to secure the personal survival of their members (by which, of course, human beings as biological organisms are as much bound as any other creatures) human societies can and do fashion a wide variety of different patterns for living. The factors which determine these changing cultural forms, with their varied emphasis on material wealth, or conquest, or religious performance are, as has already been said, complex and by no means fully understood. Certainly no single influence is at work, such as the principle of natural selection ; and, no less certainly, choice is not determined by the price of survival.

Those sociologists who have attempted to apply organic theories most literally to human societies have perhaps inadvertently done good service by the very fact that their attempted precision is self-defeating. Thus the apparent exactitude of Dr. A. G. Keller unmistakably betrays fallacies that more easily escape notice in the vaguer language of Dr. Toynbee : Dr. Keller has reduced organic analogies to the following series of parallel propositions :

> '(1) Living organisms are set down in the midst of life by conditions neither understandable nor controllable by them ; (2) they persist or disappear according as they get along, or do not get along, within their life-conditions ; (3) the whole process is one of automatic adjustment. This is organic evolution. In the hands of a science of society, the conformation is essentially the same : (1) a group of human beings—a human society—is set down in the midst of life conditions, at first neither understood nor controllable, and even in the present but poorly understood and only to a slight degree controllable : (2) the society persists or prospers according as it gets along, or does not get along, with its life conditions : (3) the whole process is predominantly one of automatic adjustment. This is societal evolution.'[1]

Unfortunately this plausible analogy is vitiated by exactly the confusions of thought which we have found to be inherent in every application to society of terms appropriate only to true biological organisms. It confuses the death of a society, in the sense of the death of actual human beings, with the modification of a particular culture-pattern : and it introduces, under cover of the objective principle of natural selection, the author's unsubstantiated theory as to the reason for such modification.

It will be noted that the very wording of the propositions itself betrays that the parallel cannot be sustained. The living organism 'persists or disappears' according as it gets along with its environment : adaptation in fact is the price of physical survival. In the second series of propositions, the word 'persists' suggests an exactly similar adaptation by the social organism, already defined as a group of human beings. Some latent uneasiness, however, as to the unreality of the physical death of a group that extends over more than one generation seems to have inhibited its rightful partner 'or disappears', for which 'or prospers' is substituted. In biological terms, however, prosperity simply means survival-plus-multiplication—and the addition of the words 'or prospers', *if they are to be read in their strict biological sense*, adds nothing to

---

[1] A. G. Keller, *Net Impressions* (Yale University Press), p. 47.

what has already been said. But to introduce an implied principle of selection by prosperity, in anything *other* than the strict biological sense, is to make an entirely unsubstantiated assumption about, not the conditions of survival, but the causes of cultural change. That such an implication is intended is apparent from the example subsequently adduced, in which Dr. Keller points out, rightly enough, that the Americans gave up slavery at about the time when it seemed likely to hinder rather than to help their material progress. The choice was slavery or riches, not slavery or death; and the Americans, for reasons in no way comparable with the imperatives of natural selection, chose riches. But even on the Western side of the Atlantic it should not be supposed that the unprosperous are under sentence of death.

None of this confusion need ever have happened if the sociologists had clearly understood the terms of reference of their own, or indeed of any, science. As we have seen, no science can make any headway at all unless it is based on exact observation of primary data and the description of these in exact language. In particular, the use of generic terms is disastrous unless the common qualities of the members of the genus are precisely defined. That has never been true of the genus 'society', round which these biological myths have been woven. Indeed, it *cannot* be true of a genus whose members, as we have seen, are so indefinite that we are unable, even when presented with a bundle of alleged specimens, accurately to distinguish one from another.

Some of the muddle might also perhaps have been avoided if sociology had not established itself as an academic discipline independent of psychology. As has already been suggested[1], the demarcation lines between academic subjects are often more than a matter of the administrative convenience of the institutions of learning in which they are studied. For the categories thus defined themselves influence the direction or even the content of thought. Around the boundaries of recognised 'subjects' there lies an undefined border-territory always imperfectly explored; and it

---

[1] See pp. 54ff.

follows that if the boundaries themselves had happened to be drawn differently, the familiar and the unfamiliar regions would have changed places. The very structure of the word 'sociology' implies that societies are a proper field of study; and its use has probably both encouraged, and been encouraged by, the fictitious life with which organic theories have sought to endow these 'societies'. Actually, what is commonly known as sociology is a part of the study of human behaviour, and should, therefore, properly rank as a branch of the general science of psychology. Since human behaviour is remarkably varied, psychology has already resolved itself into a number of specialist studies, each of which concentrates upon some particular aspect or field of behaviour. The analytical psychologist is particularly concerned with what goes on in the human mind when no one, not even the owner himself, is looking: the social psychologist is interested in observing the behaviour of human beings in association with one another; while the sociologist's special province would cover the interactions between human beings and their environment, and the relatively stable patterns of behaviour which groups of associated individuals establish over varying areas of space and time—sociology being thus a sub-division of the social branch of psychology. Such an arrangement would have the advantage of linking the sociologist to his fellow-psychologists, and, what is more important, to reality, by its emphasis on the behaviour of *actual men and women*. The only real organism known to any branch of social science is the individual human being, no matter how much some specialists may (very properly) concentrate their interest upon the behaviour of these organisms in association with one another. Zoologists who are interested in gregarious animals do not renounce their zoology to become 'agregologists'; if they did, there is no knowing what nonsense might not result. But the sociologists who keep outside the general psychological umbrella are ready victims of the temptation to go whoring after strange gods—in particular after those fictitious images that masquerade as 'social organisms'. They make a metaphor and call it science.

TESTAMENT FOR SOCIAL SCIENCE

II

The theories of Marx have been so widely popularised and have been the subject of such voluminous commentaries and glosses, explaining what Marx said, meant to say and did not mean to say, that it would be both inappropriate and unnecessary to embark upon any full discussion here. At the same time, so much sociological energy has gone down the drain as a result of the conversion of Marx's hypotheses into the system known as Marxism that it is desirable to make some attempt to sort out just what went wrong, if only as a cautionary tale with which to warn future enquirers. Moreover, and this is perhaps of even greater importance, the theories of Marx have been interpreted in a sense which if it were valid would deprive the social sciences of all claim to objectivity; and that is a conclusion which we certainly cannot afford to ignore.

Marx's own method of enquiry was, as is well known, at least fitfully empirical; the non-empirical philosophical jargon which he inherited from Hegel is only incidental. In its empirical phases Marx's work can, indeed, justly claim to rank as scientific; more than that, he was a pioneer of scientific method in the field of social affairs. The hypotheses for which he has become famous were duly based upon extensive and careful observation of actual economic and social phenomena; and, if his social surveys were carried out under the dome of the British Museum reading room rather than in streets, homes and factories, he was only using the accepted sociological tools of his age.

The hypotheses themselves which are relevant to our purposes may be reduced to three propositions—or perhaps it would be better to say to two propositions and one prophecy. The first proposition states that the way of life of any group of people at any time is mainly determined by the methods of economic production in use. The second proposition states that this influence is exercised not directly, but indirectly through the class structure of the community: the methods of production determine the class relationships and the class relationships determine everything else. And the prophecy states that, after 1848, when it was proclaimed, industrial society would divide itself more and more clearly into the two classes of the employing, property-owning bourgeoisie, and the employed (or unemployed), propertyless proletariat, everybody between these two groups being steadily ground down into the ranks of the proletarian masses. Further, this result would come about through the increasing severity of the familiar crises of capitalism, and the increasing misery that these would bring in their train.

This is not, of course, at all an adequate summary of all the theories that Marx himself put forward : there were, for instance, related doctrines about the nature of the state. But these are the central themes in his work, and the disastrous effect of Marxism upon social science can be sufficiently illustrated from them.

Provided that it is stated in a properly qualified form, none of these hypotheses need have been responsible for any such disaster. On the contrary, there is abundant evidence that the first two propositions at least contain a large measure of previously unrecognised truth : the mind which framed them must have had both the powers of observation and the imaginative insight which are the authentic marks of the great scientist. Perhaps they even entitle Marx[1] to rank as the Newton or the Darwin of social science. There is certainly plenty of empirical evidence that in politics, morals and art, as well as in more directly relevant matters, we are all inclined to take a lead from those who are supposed to be our betters : and that the classes who control the sources of our livelihood are likely at least to try to run things largely to suit themselves. Such familiar facts as the dominance in this country first of the landed gentry, then of the industrialist, and now perhaps of the trade union leader ; or the emphasis which Protestantism laid on the virtues of hard work and thrift ; or the blind

---

[1] It is, incidentally, arguable how much of the credit is due to Marx himself: it has always appeared, to me at any rate, that Engels' part was not nearly so subordinate as it is popularly reckoned to be. Engels may even, indeed, have got less than his share of the credit because he had a more agreeable personal character than Marx. However, for present purposes, we can let this question go. It is not the originators of the Marxian hypotheses, whether Marx or Engels or anyone else, who are responsible for the damage to sociology : it is on the subsequent misuse of these hypotheses that the blame must be laid.

eye which the Church of Rome has come to turn on its own condemnation of the sin of usury—these are but tiny fragments of the abundant evidence which illustrates the influence of economic conditions and class structure upon apparently non-economic aspects of social life.

It is equally clear that no fair-minded person can contend that as good a case can be made for the prophecy. On the contrary, in the past century the class hierarchy of the principal industrial countries has become more, and not less, differentiated. In England or the U.S.A. it is an entertaining, but hopeless, task to try to assign all the members of a chance collection of citizens—in a bus or cinema, a public-house or a court of law, firmly to one or other of the two great Marxian classes. The poorest wage-earners still face the richer capitalists at opposite ends of the scale, and a considerable number of small shopkeepers or manufacturers may have been bankrupted or swallowed by giant enterprises. But on the other side, we now have a greatly enlarged and much more complicated middle class, with its employed but well-paid administrators, managers, technicians, and its clerks, typists, social workers and mannequins; the proletariat is neither individually nor collectively propertyless; more, and not fewer, groups, such as midwives or patent agents, hold the recognised status of a profession; and in Britain at any rate, the wage-earners wield very considerable political power, and the relative position of the various social classes is becoming remarkably confused. Not all the sophistry in the world can pretend that 'Our own age, the bourgeois age, is distinguished by this—that it has simplified class antagonisms': or that 'more and more, society is splitting into two great hostile camps ... bourgeoisie and proletariat': or that 'those who have hitherto belonged to the lower middle class—small manufacturers, small traders, minor recipients of unearned income, handicraftsmen and peasants—slip down, one and all, into the proletariat'—which is, after all, what Marx foretold in the Communist Manifesto. If some have slipped down, others have climbed up, and there are many new intermediate positions for a growing middle class to occupy.

The chief reason for this discrepancy is one which Marx himself, if he was true to his own theories, would have respected as a proper explanation. The class structure of the main industrial countries has been modified because the technical methods of production have changed towards a pattern which demands a larger force of non-manual workers with a great variety of technical or managerial skills, some of them very highly qualified and able to exact correspondingly good pay;[1] whilst the lower ranks of wage-earners are learning to recognise the fact that, if nobody does the hard work at the bottom, we can all whistle for our livings. Further, and largely again no doubt because of the increasing political influence of the wage-earning classes, the distribution of income which would result from the undirected activities of capitalist industry has, in varying degree in different countries, been deliberately modified by taxing the well-to-do in order to guarantee, by social services, a better standard of living for the economically less fortunate.

On the remainder of the prophecy, it is perhaps prudent to suspend judgment for a while. Since Marx wrote, crises have recurred persistently, if irregularly; and if we cannot say that they have become progressively worse, we can equally not deny that in the United States, the most highly developed of all industrial countries, the crisis of the 1930's did put all that preceded it into the shade. Nevertheless, the experience of two wars, rearmament programmes and the American New Deal have given a broad hint that any government which really wanted to prevent unemployment could do so without taking the ownership and management of most of the country's industry into its own hands, provided only that it was not over-much dependent upon foreign trade. Marx naturally had to reckon without this experience; as

---

[1] It must not be inferred from this short summary that the wage or salary paid in any occupation is a simple matter of economic demand and supply: much more complicated factors of social prestige are involved which I hope to explore in a later work.

he also had to reckon without Lord Keynes's recipe for full employment in a substantially capitalist society. It may well turn out that on the subject of crises also later knowledge will prove him wrong ; but whatever there was in Marx of the genuine scientist could neither complain nor be surprised at that, since every scientist must expect his work to be superseded in time, and should know the risk that he takes if he commits himself to such specific prophecies as those of the Communist Manifesto.

Here, however, the tragedy begins—the tragedy not of Marx himself but of his effect upon the social sciences. Marx's illuminating but incomplete hypotheses had the misfortune to be translated into a 'system', with the result that for the many adherents of that system Marx must be right all the way through, not right up to a point and wrong thereafter ; and that precious effort which might have gone into constructive social research, beginning from the point where Marx left off, and employing his own empirical methods, has been wasted in proving that it is not Marx, but the facts, which are mistaken. Presently we have all the signs that science has been thrown overboard and that dogma has been crowned in its stead. There is the addition of the fatal letters 'ism and 'ist to Marx's name : there is the exaggeration and simplification of the master's teaching, the economic interpretation of history becoming not the main, but the sole, determinant of social life : there is the continued looking backward instead of forward, the search for scriptural authority, not empirical evidence, to support any new sociological hypothesis. It is true that the Marxists (unlike the Christians) do not claim divine revelation for their doctrines, but in practice this makes very little difference : keeping in line with what Stalin says that Lenin said that Marx said is much the same as keeping in line with the Bible.

The blight of Marxian dogma has long since settled over great tracts of sociological thought, for the infection has spread very widely. It has encouraged a number of natural scientists whom one might suppose to be steeped in the methods of science to adopt a curiously doctrinaire attitude towards the social sciences, and to quite uncritical admiration of the achievements of the Soviet Union. Even in this country it has occasionally distorted the natural scientist's attitude towards his own specialism, as when so eminent a biologist as Professor J. B. S. Haldane can write that 'until I studied Marxism I used to write of the balance between mutation and selection'[1]—as though Marx's idea could be relevant to the correct expression of a subject of which he had never heard. And, of course, so long as Marxism remains the official philosophy of the Soviet Union, it not only completely frustrates the potential contribution of a great people to genuine social research, but produces the ludicrous spectacle of contemporary biologists using the 'classics of Marxism' to put Darwin to rights.[2] Of the two great superstitions of the Western world—Christianity and Marxism—Christianity has, of course, had a much longer period in which to sterilise fine intelligences and divert the most powerful instrument that we know—the human mind—from fruitful use in the service of the species which possess it; but in the present generation it is hard to say which of the two carries the heavier burden of guilt on that particular account.

The Marxist philosophy, moreover, easily gives colour to an insidious determinism which would render all sociological research futile; for, if the politics, the religion and the art of any epoch merely reflect the attitudes of the social class which, thanks to the prevailing methods of production, occupies the seats of power, the same will be true of the findings of the social researchers. It follows that no permanent, objectively valid, laws can ever be established in social science—except only, of course, the law that formulates the materialist interpretation of history itself.

Like all the main hypotheses suggested by Marx, this kind of social relativity theory contains substantial elements of truth, to which large concessions can and should be made. In the first place, we may concede that most of us most of the time think the thoughts, just as much as we use the language, of our age. But it

---

[1] *Science and Everyday Life* by J. B. S. Haldane, F.R.S. (Pelican Books), p. 172.
[2] *Soviet Biology* by T. D. Lysenko (Birch Books), p. 8.

must not be forgotten that in relation to social matters, most of us are, as has already been pointed out, still living in a state of pre-scientific darkness ; and at all times the capacity both to perceive and to transcend these limitations will demand a degree both of insight and of intellectual discipline which are perhaps never likely to be very common qualities, though that is not to say that they are unattainable.

Secondly, it is clear that the focus of interest varies from age to age and that, therefore, the direction of social enquiries is likely to be influenced by particular circumstances of time and place : even, we may admit, by the particular needs of whatever is the ruling class. That, however, is no less true of the natural sciences ; and in neither physical nor social research does the choice of the line of enquiry to be pursued have anything to do with the rightness or the wrongness of the results that are reached. It has repeatedly been pointed out how the bent of the natural sciences has accommodated itself to the practical requirements of various epochs. It was the primitive agriculturist's need to keep careful watch on the seasons which fostered the growth of astronomy : in our own age it is hard to believe that so much care would have been lavished on atomic research, if the expected results had had purely peaceful uses ; and it is obvious that, even in medical science, more attention is given in the Western world to research into the causes of cancer than to beri-beri. Similarly, in the social sciences it is natural that research into trade cycles should be more impressively endowed in the United States than are enquiries into the distribution of the national income.

In the third place, the social scientist, like his colleagues in the natural sciences, can, of course, only draw upon experience which is available to him. In the case of the natural scientist this limitation means for the most part that he cannot anticipate the findings of later workers. That, indeed, is an obvious consequence of the progressive nature of scientific research. Aristotle could have nothing to say about molecules, and what Lucretius thought about atoms is not now much to the point. Yet the nature of matter or the qualities of space-time must presumably have been much the same in the days of ancient Greece and Rome as they are now. Ignorance of discoveries not yet made is not, however, the only limitation upon experience : there is also the possibility that the actual phenomena in which the scientist is interested may themselves be modified in course of time. Even the natural sciences are not wholly free from limitations of this kind : in the study of plant or animal life, for instance, new ecological patterns are continually emerging, and no one can observe the biological effects of a mutation which has not yet occurred. In the social sciences these limitations are particularly severe, for social phenomena are more constantly subject to such changes, and the changes themselves are apt to be both more rapid and more radical than is usual in the phenomena studied by the natural scientists. Plato could not have said anything, except by way of imaginative prophecy, about the problems of industrialised societies, for the relevant data had not, up to his time, ever existed.

Finally, we must recognise, and this perhaps brings us right to the heart of the matter, that many social scientists have formulated laws in terms which do suggest that these are much more widely applicable than in fact is true. In this connection the supposedly universal truths enunciated by the classical economists of the nineteenth century leap to the mind. The demographic calculations of Malthus, the iron law of wages and the theories of the mercantilists have all suffered a sad decline since they were first sprung upon the world.[1] And they have so suffered, not merely because, like scientific hypotheses generally, they have been corrected and supplemented by later works, but also because they all in some degree rested upon concealed premises, which were later dragged into the pitiless light of day : they were all at best partially true in particular conditions the universality of which was implicitly, and quite incorrectly, assumed. And for that reason they were an easy prey for the Marxist out to show that objective generalisations about human affairs (other than those contained in Marxism) are

---

[1]though it could be argued that, in slightly modified versions, all three are now creeping back into favour.

only a will o' the wisp, if not indeed one of the many deliberate frauds perpetuated by the ruling classes for their own advantage.

It is, however, one thing to claim for an hypothesis a degree of generality to which it is not entitled, and quite another to dismiss all limited generalisations as futile. Precise knowledge of the causes and cures of unemployment in the conditions of twentieth-century America is not to be despised because it throws little light on the social organisation of the Pygmies or has less general relevance than a knowledge of the law of gravity. The movements of currents and tides along a particular coast can be charted by careful local observation, even by those who have no knowledge of the underlying geographical principles; and he would be a rash sailor who would reject such a chart because of its restricted scope. The social scientist must, in fact, often plead guilty to having failed to notice the implicit premises which limit the range of his conclusions; but he need not and does not admit the charge that, even when that limitation is clearly recognised, his work is scientifically negligible.

Nor must we jump to the conclusion that, because much social research is relevant only to particular cultural conditions, no wider generalisations can ever be possible. The physical resemblances between members even of widely separated branches of the human species are much more striking than their differences: the physiologist does not have to write separate textbooks for Negro and for Chinese physiology. It would be odd, indeed, if there were not comparable uniformities in the human mind which psychological science could express in terms of equal generality. On the other hand, it is not surprising if such laws take a good deal of finding, or if we are long confined to limited and partial statements. For whatever its common elements, the human mind is clearly a most flexible instrument: the range of patterns of both individual and collective behaviour which it has already produced needs no emphasis. Hence, as always in the human sciences, it is the complexity and variety of the conditions in which observations must be made which make it difficult to detect any underlying uniformities. That, however, must not be taken as evidence that no such uniformities exist. After all, it would not be easy to arrive at the law of gravity from observation of the movement of motor vehicles in Piccadilly or Fifth Avenue : and two observers untrained in science, one of whom had spent a lifetime studying the effects of hookworm in the West Indies, whilst the other had made a similar study of frostbite in the Arctic, might, even if they exchanged experiences, find it difficult to arrive at the common physiological laws which contain the key to both their problems.

Nor, again, should we surrender to the pessimistic conclusion that all of us are always so blinkered by our own ephemeral environment that we must give up every hope of distinguishing between the local and temporal on the one hand, and the universal on the other. The detached and objective observation which is the basis of all scientific method has never been an easy art to practise : in every field it has had to fight against the obstacles of established mental habit, prejudice, superstitition and vested interest. But with every victory the techniques become more familiar and better established. There is no reason why the social scientist's peculiar difficulty of getting his own experience into due perspective should not be overcome as much as any of these other obstructions : indeed, the work of the social anthropologists in exploring the effects of cultural conditions upon personality and attitude are already an object-lesson in what can be achieved in this way. Moreover, there are strong forces at work to make the blinkers less effective than they used to be. Even a century ago there were excuses which would not pass muster today for not seeing beyond one's nose. For the volume of comparative experience increases steadily, and what is more important, it becomes daily more accessible and better recorded. As the ages in which 'mankind has thrown away most of its experience'[1] recede, there need be no lack of checks by which we can ourselves correct (or others can correct for us) possible local distortions of our observations.

---

[1] See p. 12.

In any case, the economic interpretation of history, when stretched to deny the possibility of objective social science, proves too much. Like all determinist theories, it is hoist with its own petard. For if all hypotheses about human affairs are firmly conditioned by the economic and social environment in which they are made, that must be true equally of the Marxian theory itself. Marx and his followers must be as much the creatures of their time and circumstance as anybody else; although they always, of course, implicitly make an exception for their own doctrines. We have, therefore, only to pluck up courage to poke the bogeyman which they have created, and we shall find that there is nothing there.

CHAPTER FIVE

SCIENCE AND METAPHYSICS

I

THE birth of the social sciences suggests that the time has come to re-examine the question whether there are any limitations upon the potential conquests of science which look as if they must be permanent, and which cannot be explained by the pre-scientific mental climate of our age or the wrong turnings taken by misguided social scientists. The three provinces which most commonly claim to be thus inaccessible to scientific method are those of metaphysics, morals and the arts. In all three, though less elaborately in the third, religious doctrines which claim both to explain the nature of the universe and to find divine sanction for man's notions of goodness and beauty, have staked out a rival claim to rule. In all three I shall suggest that science has a much larger part to play than is yet generally recognised.

Metaphysical theories which profess to explain the nature of the universe, without passing judgment upon it or moralising about it, clearly resemble the hypotheses of science in just this fact that they are purely explanatory. But, unlike the hypotheses of science, they conspicuously fail to rise steadily upon one another's shoulders towards ever more comprehensive generalisations. 'The science of today will look as foolish in a century's time as that of a century ago does now, and with as good a reason ... In comparison the theories of the philosophers have perennial youth'.[1] The theologians do not regard the work of St. Augustine or Thomas Aquinas as superseded by the later discoveries of Cardinal Newman and Archbishop Temple; nor is the relationship of St.

---
[1] Ritchie, *Scientific Method*, p. 14.

Francis to St. Paul that of Einstein to Newton. Progress is blocked wherever conclusive empirical proof or disproof is impossible; and theories not subject to such verification are, therefore, permanently stuck at the hypothetical stage. No metaphysician has finally refuted any other metaphysician in matters that cannot be settled by the evidence of the senses or by primitive psychological experience. If he could, the theories of the philosophers would lose their perennial youth, and the progress of metaphysical knowledge would begin. Since he cannot, metaphysics can only move in a circle, not, like science, in a spiral; and the age-long battles between idealist and materialist can rage forever without either combatant being effectively driven from the field.

This remains true even though certain philosophical theories are in fact, by common consent discarded in the light of later knowledge. No one now believes with Thales that everything is made of water. But it is significant that such progressive amendment is applicable only to a particular type of philosophical theory, namely, those which deal with matters susceptible of empirical observation. Philosophical doctrines of this kind (as distinct from, say, those which postulate direct non-sensory apprehension of the existence of God) are in effect genuinely scientific theories, in the special sense in which that word was used in Chapter II; for they offer comprehensive hypotheses which bring into one general statement many otherwise unrelated laws of association between empirical events. They are thus concerned with natural, not with supernatural, phenomena.

Further—and this is the important point—even these theories have no capacity for growth within themselves. Comprehensive philosophical doctrines about, say, the nature of matter are finally disproved only by the results of *scientific* investigation and only in the fields in which the methods of science can be, and are, employed. If the philosophers commit themselves to hypotheses which are subject to empirical verification, then these hypotheses, like all other scientific theories, must be consistent with the rest of the knowledge about sensory and psychological data which has been accumulated by the various sciences. Metaphysical doctrines are, therefore, liable to become obsolete, not as a result of the progress of metaphysics, but simply because the philosopher and the theologian must not contradict the progressive discoveries of science, if only for the excellent reason that, if they do, nobody will pay any attention to what they say. Such doctrines yield in fact to the external pressure of the progress of science, but remain incapable of advancing under their own steam : primitive brute experience has still the last word. Thus, in the face of modern biological knowledge, the theory that God has created and sustains the world can no longer stand in the form in which it appears in the book of Genesis ; whereas the hypothesis of the deity as emergent evolution remains tenable, but is equally insusceptible of proof or disproof, so long as it runs into no similar conflict with science. In short, in so far as the works of St. Augustine and St. Thomas Aquinas have become definitely obsolete, it is scientists such as Darwin or Freud, not any later theologians, who are responsible. Incidentally, this is almost equivalent to saying that metaphysical theories are only certain of survival so long as they are also metaphorical ; in which case, however, it can also be argued that they have no meaning.

The interesting point here is the implied recognition of the unique status of scientific research as the sole foundation of solid knowledge. Even the modern theological doctrine of progressive revelation is itself an admission of the progressive nature of science and the static nature of theology. For, according to this doctrine, science is itself a continuous revelation of the works of God. The Creator has endowed human creatures with powers of scientific observation and inference in order that they may use these faculties to acquire understanding of his handiwork. It is true that this doctrine involves theological difficulties (discussed in the section that follows), and true also that, in order to meet these difficulties, counter-claims are often advanced on behalf of extra-scientific revelation which go far to nullify the respect for science implied by the concept of progressive revelation. Nevertheless that concept is itself an admission that it is to the sciences ordinarily so called that even the theologian must look if he is to enlarge the boundaries of his own peculiar province of knowledge. In short, while science perpetually revises its own conclusions, it is on science also that philosophy and theology must depend for the revision of theirs.

II

Those philosophers whose speculations are untrammelled by religious dogmas can cheerfully give unqualified recognition to the supremacy of science. In so far as their metaphysical theories are capable of empirical proof, or, as more frequently happens, of empirical *dis*proof by science, they can enjoy, though they do not themselves contribute to, the upward progression towards more solid and comprehensive knowledge which is the scientist's particular delight. At the same time, in cases where no such verification is possible, the sceptical philosopher has no need to claim for his theories anything more than the status of plausible hypotheses; and he certainly will not accord a higher rank than this to any proposition put forward by his colleagues in contradiction of his own. In ordinary life he will, no doubt, distinguish clearly enough between the firm knowledge derived from sensory experience and the unsubstantiated speculations of his own profession. Whatever his views about the nature of matter, he will, like the rest of us, normally try to avoid stepping in front of a moving vehicle. But since his opinions on issues that cannot be settled by scientific proof do not have to be squared with anything else, the undogmatic, untheological philosopher has no need to deny their permanently hypothetical nature. He at least can enjoy the pleasures of perennial youth without mistaking them for the wisdom of advancing years.

It should be emphasised that in this context 'undogmatic philosopher' means just what it says; that is to say, simply one who does not claim the status of knowledge for anything other than the laws of science: it includes, therefore, the genuine agnostic who neither asserts nor denies the existence of God, but takes the view that there is no conclusive evidence on either side. I stress this point, since it is sometimes argued that on this particular topic, suspension of judgment is impossible. No agnostic position, it is said, is tenable, since one must either categorically assert or categorically (though not necessarily explicitly) deny the reality of God. In the words of Sir Walter Moberly:

> 'Whoever rules the theologian out of court as an academic thinker or teacher, simply on the ground that he is a committed man, should first scrutinize his own position and mark the unproved assumption which he himself is making. His position would be reasonable only if any claim that there has been a self-revelation of God in history could be dismissed dogmatically as inherently incredible, before examination of the evidence. But that would be to beg the whole question at issue between the Christian and the unbeliever. But if the claim can be admitted as a hypothesis to be examined, then, on that hypothesis, the humble, receptive and "committed" attitude of the theologian would be reasonable. In any case commitment one way or other is unavoidable. Suspense of judgment is an illusion, since it is impossible to suspend living. Throughout his thinking, the student of theological questions is actually living either a godward or a godless life. There is no third alternative. The true obscurantist then, as we have already urged, is the man who claims to be without presuppositions and therefore never criticizes those which he has. Therein very possibly he fools his neighbours, and certainly he fools himself'.[1]

Such an attempt to rule out the true sceptic and to divide us all into dogmatic believers and dogmatic unbelievers involves a confusion between knowledge and action. In practical life it is constantly necessary to act on the assumption that one hypothesis is more likely to be right than another, without in the least committing ourselves to firm belief in either. For instance, when you go out, you must either take your umbrella or leave it at home : when it comes to action there is indeed no third choice. Which alternative you choose depends on whether you *think* it is more likely to rain or not to rain ; but whichever course you take, you are very well aware that in the British climate in the present state of meteorological knowledge, you are quite likely to be wrong, and you claim nothing more than the status of an hypo-

---

[1] *The Crisis in the University* by Sir Walter Moberly (S.C.M. Press), p. 287.

thesis for your opinion. Although you must act on one assumption or the other, you retain, in fact, a genuine intellectual doubt as to which is correct.

Such a position is strictly parallel to that of the truly agnostic philosopher who openly admits that he sees no evidence sufficient either to prove or disprove the existence of God, but who is as much obliged to lead either a 'godward or a godless' life as any of us is obliged either to carry, or not to carry, an umbrella. If you can be an agnostic about the weather, you can equally well be an agnostic about God. There are, indeed, only two significant differences between the two cases. In the first place, an hypothesis about the weather on a particular date will be ultimately subject to empirical verification, so that we have the eventual satisfaction of knowing whether we were right or wrong. That satisfaction (in this life at any rate) is not open to the agnostic in religion. In the second place, since worship of, or communion with, a deity of whose existence one is not absolutely convinced, is likely to be an unsatisfying experience, the agnostic will generally *act upon* the hypothesis that there is no God. It is, in fact, the believer, and not, as Sir Walter suggests, the unbeliever, who requires absolute conviction; for the believer's religion turns to dust and ashes unless he is utterly certain that the God whom he worships is real, and that those who deny this are wrong. But the unbeliever remains just what this word implies—one who, whichever way his own opinion inclines, holds that, as with the weather, there is insufficient evidence for a firm conclusion either way.

Clearly, then, science cannot give the believer the certain conviction which is essential for his religion. It follows that if you want to claim more for your interpretation of the universe than the rank of unproven intellectual hypothesis, you must base your claim not on science, but on a faith that is derived from extra-scientific sources of knowledge. The theologian, therefore, is necessarily more grudging than the sceptical philosopher in his recognition of the supremacy of science. He cannot allow science the last word every time, or recognise, as can the agnostic, that questions on which science has not yet spoken must be treated as still open.

For extra-scientific knowledge the theologian turns to revelation, drawing (if he is a Christian) both upon the 'special revelation' contained in the historical events of the life of Christ, and upon the general revelation of God to the mind of man. We may consider first the relation of science to special revelation. The evidence for any historical religion, since it is part of history, is, of course, at least at one level accessible to scientific method. In the case of Christianity, the evidence for the life of Christ is a matter of record. Since the events to which the record relates occurred many years ago, and no absolutely contemporary account of them survives, the evidence is necessarily second or third hand; but the weight of testimony about the life of Jesus Christ is such that his existence as an historical person is not in dispute. What is disputed is, of course, the doctrine that Christ was the son of God, and therefore more than human, and that his incarnation and life were an expression of God's concern for the redemption of mankind. The evidence for this doctrine rests partly upon the miracles described in the Gospel stories, and partly upon the testimony of believers throughout the Christian era who assert that they have unmistakable spiritual apprehension of the divinity of Jesus.

The interesting point about the miraculous part of this evidence is that, although the worker of miracles demonstrates an ability to override the known laws of science, yet, as proof of this ability, he offers strictly sensory evidence. The doctrine that seeing is believing is the basic foundation on which all scientific knowledge rests. If, therefore, you wish to establish some fact which apparently conflicts with the teachings of science, you are in an exceptionally strong position if you can rest your claim on that very same foundation. On this account the churches are, no doubt, wise to cling as long as possible to the authenticity of the Christian miracles. If the facts are as recorded, the proof of Christ's ability miraculously to multiply the loaves and fishes is strictly sensory:

it is, in fact, the physical presence of those extra loaves and fishes. And the proof, at this level, of the resurrection, is equally sensory: it is the disappearance, in circumstances otherwise unexplained, of Christ's body from the tomb and his reappearance later before the eyes of the disciples. No scientist can ignore sensory data without undermining the whole body of scientific knowledge, since the validity of this knowledge rests upon scrupulous regard for every relevant sensory observation, and unflinching refusal to pick and choose between convenient and inconvenient sense-data.

Alleged miracles are rare. A miracle is, however, just one example of a visible, audible or tangible breakdown of laws of association that previously appeared to be reliable. Such an apparent breakdown is not in itself an altogether uncommon occurrence. For instance, after biological research appeared to have established firmly enough that acquired characters are not inherited, some observers produced what looked like contrary evidence. The children of rats which had been trained to run through mazes were found to make their way through mazes more readily than the children of rats not similarly experienced. And the Soviet biologist Lysenko[1] has asserted that, according to his experiments, if a scion of one variety of tomato is grafted on to a stock of another variety, some of the offspring of the stock will show characters typical of the grafted scion.

Whenever science is faced with such an apparent breakdown of established laws of association, there is only one thing to be done —that is, of course, to repeat, in as strictly controlled conditions as are possible, the observations which produced the exceptional instance. This usually settles the matter fairly quickly in one way or another. The anomalous observation may turn out to have been quite simply wrong, in which case the breakdown is, of course, purely imaginary. Or the observer may have overlooked some factor which makes the peculiar case not strictly comparable with those with which it has been compared. The rats, for instance,

---

[1] In his Address to the All-Union Lenin Academy of Agricultural Sciences, Moscow, 1948. See *Soviet Biology* (Birch Books).

who did well at their lessons in the first generation may have been exceptionally clever, and what they handed down to their children may have been not acquired skill, but native wit, or exceptional ability to acquire skills. The peculiarities of Lysenko's tomato plants may not be characters inherited by the seeds of the stock from the scion; they may be symptoms of a disease developed by the offspring of the stock in its own lifetime. In such cases also, of course, the breakdown is imaginary. Alternatively, it may be that the previously established law is genuinely shaken by the new data. If repeated observations should show that acquired characters are in some circumstances inherited, there must be hitherto unrecognised limitations to the rule that they are not heritable. Further research must then be directed to finding out just what those limitations are, so that the rule may be restated in a form which is not disturbed by any known exceptions. That, after all, is the characteristic process by which science advances. Unfortunately, however, in the case of alleged miracles of some two thousand years' standing, repeated observations and experiments are not practicable. The scientist, therefore, can pronounce no final judgment—except to say that the evidence for the Christian miracles has not passed the observational tests that he would normally require before accepting such startling exceptions to well-established laws of science.

Christians do not, however, rely only on physical miracles: some of them, even, like the Bishop of Birmingham[1], are virtually renouncing these miracles altogether. The Christian faith depends even more closely upon extra-scientific 'revelation', the evidence for which is the testimony of those to whom the revelation has been made. In this respect Christianity is of a piece with all theistic explanations of the universe, except that the Christian enjoys not only the 'general' revelation of God to man, but also the 'special' revelation of the Christian story. According to Canon Richardson: 'Revelation is miraculous and comes by miraculous means—by the gift of prophetic inspiration, by the divine opening

---

[1] See below, pp. 111 ff.

of our eyes to the truth, by the mysterious awakening of faith . . . Revelation is thus not the rational deduction of truth (the *revelatum*) from certain given premises (assured to us by *revelatio*), nor yet is it a scientific induction which results in the framing of a "most probable hypothesis" . . . Men do not arrive at faith through being convinced on rational grounds of the validity of a theistic philosophy ; they arrive at Christian theism because they first had some gift of faith'.[1] Acceptance of the truth of such revelation thus implies also acceptance of the proposition that our knowledge is derived from two distinct sources, and consists on the one hand of truths revealed to direct spiritual apprehension, and, on the other hand, of inferences drawn by scientific method from the observations of primitive sense-experience.

The knowledge which is supposed to be derived from revelation differs, it should be noted, in several important particulars from that which is based on science. In the first place, revealed knowledge lacks the universality which we have found to be an essential quality of the sensory and psychological data in which all scientific knowledge is grounded. Sight and hearing are experiences coextensive with mankind, independent of everything except the possession of eyes and ears. Revelation, on the other hand, though widespread, is far from universal ; for it must be remembered that revelation, if it is to rank as an independent extra-scientific source of knowledge, means something more than the emotions of awe or exaltation with which it is associated : it means those emotions, *plus* the overwhelming certainty of communion with God, and consequent conviction of his existence. A very considerable part of the human race shows no sign of having this experience in its totality. Certainly, the number of whom this is true is now far too great to be dismissed as the spiritual equivalent of the negligible minority who go through life physically blind or deaf.

Secondly, there is another sense in which revealed knowledge lacks the universality of the data of science. For the content of all revelations is by no means the same : the Almighty, it seems, has

---

[1] *Christian Apologetics* by Alan Richardson (S.C.M. Press), p. 166.

divulged different versions of the truth to different people, if not indeed to different peoples. Revealed knowledge cannot, therefore, be universal, because it is not consistent : you cannot believe all of it at once; whereas the laws of association which science currently believes to be true must, by definition, be compatible with one another. More than a century ago Robert Owen remarked at the early age of ten upon this inconsistency in the 'truths' apprehended by the act of faith, and decided accordingly to have done with religion, on the ground that if the various religions were in such violent conflict, it seemed probable that there must be something fundamentally wrong with them all.

Notwithstanding these significant differences between the respective data of science and of revelation, those who accept revelation as a source of knowledge normally insist that its content is something very much better established than one of a number of possible hypotheses about the nature of the universe. The absolute character of faith is, indeed, its third point of difference from the knowledge derived from science. The believer *knows* that God exists, and that communion between the divine mind and his own spirit is real. It is true that the long and bloody fight for religious toleration has now brought us to a point at which the faithful no longer dispute the agnostic argument that, in the absence of any scientific proof such as would generally be acceptable to both parties, theism based on revelation or religious experience is an hypothesis the truth of which *cannot* be demonstrated to those who have not had that experience. But this is not accepted by the believer himself as evidence that his hypothesis is actually doubtful : he still claims that he at least *knows* the truth by faith, though there may be many others too blind to see it. The whole attitude to doubt is, indeed, a critical test of the difference between faith and scientific knowledge. The believer must not keep an open mind, ready to abandon his faith should the weight of evidence seem to point that way. To the faithful doubt is a sin : to the scientist it is the first of all virtues. To appreciate the width of the gulf between them, one only has to match the spectacle of the Christian 'fighting hard for his belief' with a parallel image of the scientist wrestling with his soul in the laboratory in a struggle to remain unconvinced by the evidence of nuclear fission. It may be true that men of science acquire a vested interest in their own theories, so that they may be reluctant, for instance, to see the work of a lifetime superseded by later discoveries : hence Darwin's practice of noting with special care evidence which ran counter to his theories. But, as Darwin's example shows, to resist doubt is the scientist's temptation—and the believer's triumph.

A religious interpretation of the universe implies, therefore, that we have two distinct sources of knowledge—science and revelation—one of which is accepted by believers and unbelievers alike, and one of which has been revealed to some but not to others. Provided that revelation does not deal with the same phenomena as science, and does not produce accounts of these which contradict those reached by scientific method, the scientist is, of course, in no position categorically to deny the claim of revelation to rank as a source of knowledge. He is, however, bound to emphasise the universality of his own data in contrast with the limited and contradictory character of what is revealed ; and it is surely also his business to insist that revelation, like his own laws, must be treated (which in practice it is not) as at best an hypothesis completely open to modification in the light of later knowledge. Further, it is difficult to understand how a scientist, while refusing in all other spheres to commit himself to conclusions, except as the result of inductive inference from precise observation of empirical phenomena, can yet be prepared to dogmatise without any real evidence about the nature of things. If he does so, it is, as we have seen in Chapter III, at the risk of encouraging contra-scientific attitudes of mind which too often have been used, and still may be used, to thwart the realisation of the magnificent potentialities of his own work.

Certainly, no one who respects the methods of science can admit the recent astonishing attempt of theology to steal the prestige of science by claiming itself to rank as an empirical science in its own right. This claim has been pressed on three principal grounds by Canon Richardson, and similar arguments which are discussed below have been used by Sir Walter Moberly in defence of the claim of (Christian) theology to a place in University teaching. Canon Richardson[1] adduces as evidence first, the 'independent use' which theology (in common with other sciences) makes of its own 'categories' of scientific classification and interpretation: second, the use made by theologians of scientific method: and third the 'scientific spirit' in which the theologian approaches his task.

To deal in turn with the points raised in this argument, we may observe that a great deal hangs on this slippery word 'category' which is not precisely defined in Canon Richardson's book. In relation to the natural sciences, 'category' seems to mean an hypothetical theory in the sense in which I have used that word in Chapter II of this essay. Some biologists, for instance, according to Canon Richardson, admit the category of progress but deny the validity of a category of purpose in biological science: 'mechanism' and 'evolution' are also used as illustrations of categories, along with the 'projections' and 'father-complexes' of the psychologists. The significance of these categories, it appears, is that they confer a kind of monopoly upon the workers in any particular science, since these workers and these alone are competent to criticise their own categories. 'Criticism and modification must come from within and not from without the particular scientific discipline itself, since those who venture to criticise from outside, however eminent they may be in some other field, have not the technical competence to make a judgment.' 'Helpful co-operation' can, indeed, in Canon Richardson's view, take place between different sciences, as for instance psychology and anthropology, even when they are looking at the same phenomena from their own distinctive points of view, provided always that 'one

---

[1] *Christian Apologetics* by Alan Richardson (S.C.M. Press), pp. 55 ff.

science abstains from upholding dogmatically hypotheses which stultify the categories of the other'.[1]

It may be remarked in passing that no science that deserved the name could uphold any hypothesis *dogmatically*, the expression being, indeed, a contradiction in terms; and one is tempted further to wonder what progress chemistry would have made, if in the past century the physicists had respected this warning to keep out of the chemists' territory. The explanation of Canon Richardson's extreme departmentalism appears, however, when on the one hand he rebukes the psychologists for 'trying to explain away the categories of theological science by reducing the latter to categories of their own',[2] such as projections and so forth; and on the other hand it turns out that the special 'category' of theological science is revelation.[3] This is, indeed, a remarkable piece of sophistry. To the biologist or psychologist such 'categories' as progress, evolution, unconscious mind or projection are genuine hypotheses, derived from the observation of primitive empirical data, and ready to be thrown overboard without damage to the science as a whole if they prove incompatible with later observations in the field of biology, psychology or any other science. But, of course, the theologian's category of revelation is something quite different: it is not a provisional empirical hypothesis at all, but a fundamental assumption without which the whole alleged 'science' of theology must collapse. All genuine sciences, as we have seen, begin from empirical observations, and then, as knowledge increases in their own or in related fields, move steadily from one hypothesis to another in order to establish laws of association between the phenomena observed. The successively discarded hypotheses are the bricks of which the science is built. Theology, on the other hand, receives a 'revelation' falsely labelled as an hypothesis, and makes this the irremovable foundation stone of its whole 'science', by issuing explicit instructions that it is on

---

[1] *Ibid*, p. 56.
[2] *Ibid*, p. 42.
[3] "Theology as a science stands or falls with the category of revelation' . . ., *Ibid*, p. 57.

no account to be touched by non-theologians. No wonder that Canon Richardson is determined that no one from outside should criticise the theologian's special 'category'; for, if it can be shown that the phenomena which he studies (such as religious emotion) can be adequately explained by biological and psychological hypotheses, the 'science' of theology is gone: or more accurately, it is shown up as the plain dogmatism that it is. The argument, therefore, that theology is a science because it has its own categories, and that these must be immune from external criticism, simply amounts to imposing dogma under pretence of hypothesis.

One wonders if the theologians have considered how dangerously this argument might be used in other contexts. The astrologers, for instance, clearly have their own categories of interpretation of the relation between the movement of heavenly bodies and human affairs. They have only to assert that no one outside the ranks of astrologers is 'competent to make a judgment' on the validity of these categories, for the 'science' of astrology to be established on a foundation identical with that on which Canon Richardson rests his claim for the validity of theological science, and, indeed, for the truth of the Christian religion.[1]

The second strand in Canon Richardson's thesis, that theology is an empirical science, would not, taken by itself and at its face value, be open to any objection. 'By theology we here mean the study of Christian existence in history and today, that is, of *all*[2] that appertains to the believing and witnessing Christian community, the Church, both in the past and in the present . . . The science of theology is rendered necessary by the existence of the Church, just as the existence of physical objects makes necessary the science of physics.' Provided always that the theologians are

---

[1] The whole argument of Canon Richardson's book could, indeed, be very easily transposed to prove the truth of astrology. 'It cannot be too strongly stressed', he writes (footnote to p. 137) 'that the Church's own life and witness are the true apology for the Christian faith. The story of the Church's expansion and activity during the last century and a half and in our own days constitutes as impressive a record of victorious living as anything which previous centuries can show'. The astrologers can also produce a considerable body of followers, if that is all that is necessary to establish the truth of a belief.

[2] *Ibid*, p. 50 (Italics mine).

prepared open-mindedly to study *all* the phenomena related to the Church, and to do so without reservations or inhibiting dogmatic categories such as revelation, the Christian Church would be an entirely proper subject for scientific examination.

In order to prove that the theologians have, in fact, the necessary scientific objectivity and freedom from dogma, Canon Richardson makes his third point, about 'the scientific spirit in which the theologian approaches his task'.[1] This involves proving that a closed mind is an open one. The argument here runs as follows: An open mind is never really as open as it looks: no scientist ever approaches his task with a mind that is completely open. Even scientists 'must believe in the unity and uniformity of things, in the value of knowledge, the importance of their subject, and so on'.[2] The theologian also 'like every other scientist, must come to his work with a high regard for its dignity and value, a deep sense of vocation, lofty standards of intellectual integrity and an earnest desire to know the truth'.[3] That much, indeed, is indisputable: but the next stage in the argument involves an astonishing *non sequitur*. 'Since the theologian must come to his subject with a high regard for its dignity and value, it follows in practice—*if not absolutely in theory*—that he will be a convinced member of the believing and witnessing Christian community. Where else will he acquire the sense of the dignity and value of his science, save in the Christian Church? Apart from his life in the Church, he will have no direct knowledge of the *data* of his enquiry.'[3] In other words, you cannot make a scientific study of the phenomena of the Christian Church and religion unless you are already convinced that the beliefs of that Church are true. By the same token one could argue that an anthropologist could not make a scientific study of some primitive community unless he shared the religious and other beliefs—many of which he would normally regard as superstitious—of that community. The implicit moral seems to be

---

[1] *Ibid*, p. 60.
[2] *Ibid*, p. 60.
[3] *Ibid*, p. 61. (Italics mine)

that, unless a theologian is a convinced Christian, his open-minded studies of Christian experience *might* lead him to the opinion that the Christians were also the victims of superstitious beliefs: on that subject therefore his open mind must be closed in advance.

Sir Walter Moberly's argument in defence of the teaching of Christian theology in our Universities runs on closely parallel lines. Sir Walter is, however, so fair-minded that he states the case against himself in terms which his own subsequent argument quite fails to shake. 'On our own showing,' he writes as Devil's advocate, 'a Faculty of Theology has not an open mind; it does not ask, but begs, the ultimate questions . . . In the university, whose essential principle is to follow the argument whithersoever it leads, it is intellectual treason. In effect the Faculty says to the individual theological teacher, "Enquire as pertinaciously, weigh evidence as meticulously, apply scientific canons as rigorously as you please so long as you do so within the prescribed limit. Transgress that limit, carry the same methods and the same caution in coming to conclusions beyond it, and you will be struck off the roll" . . . No British University would think of accepting a Chair for the propagation of Marxist Economics, of Logical Positivism, of Whig History, or of Mendelian Biology.'[1] The position could hardly be more accurately described.

Sir Walter's own answer to this dilemma is simply to contend in terms of the passage which we have already quoted[2] that everybody must be committed one way or the other on the subject of religious belief. That, however, as we have seen, is not a true picture. It is perfectly possible to study the phenomena of religious experience without holding any opinions on the subject which are dogmatic in the sense that, being derived from faith and not from science, they must be retained whatever the result of such study. The Christian faith is one possible hypothesis which may explain some of these phenomena. But the university which appoints a professor of Christian Theology is conferring on this particular

---

[1] *The Crisis in the University* (S.C.M. Press), pp. 283, 284.
[2] See p. 97.

interpretation of the religious experience the status not of hypothesis, but of dogma, and is quite patently guilty of the 'intellectual treason' of refusing in advance 'to follow the argument whithersoever it leads'. The parallel of Mendelian Biology is, indeed, dangerously apt. Universities do not appoint professors of Mendelian Biology because they appreciate that Mendel's theories may be modified or superseded by later discoveries, and they do not wish to pay professors to teach theories which have been shown to be incomplete or incorrect. If they appoint professors of Christian Theology, they are by implication refusing to face the possibility that the Christian hypothesis may be false. No conceivable subtleties of reasoning can obscure the plain fact that the attitude of the Christian to his faith is fundamentally different from the attitude of the scientist to his hypothesis. It is indeed precisely true that the Christian theologian must, in Sir Walter's own words, attempt to 'apply scientific canons' only 'within the prescribed limit', while the true scientist recognises no limits. No conceivable subtleties of reasoning, in fact, can prove that closed minds are open or open minds closed.

III

I doubt if the Christians would have shown such eagerness to usurp the name of science, or to deny to the scientist the possibility of an open mind, if they were not engaged in a fierce rearguard action. That they adopt this attitude is another remarkable testimony to the prestige of science and, I think, a significant hint of where ultimate victory will lie. It is indeed sometimes suggested, particularly from the side of religion, that the nineteenth-century debate between science and religion was an exaggerated fuss arising from misunderstandings which have since been amicably composed. Science and religion, it is said, deal with different fields, or at the very least with different aspects, of experience; and each can afford to respect the other's province. All the squabbling of the past was due to failure to realise this, with the result that each party inadvertently trespassed into the territory of the other; but it can now be recognised that this was all due to an unfortunate mistake.

'It is true that a century ago, in face of advancing scientific discoveries, misconceived defence of the Bible's inerrancy precipitated a landslide of incredulity across the trunk road to Christian belief . . . Clerical obscurantism in the past did much harm. So also did the rashness with which some scientists dismissed as untenable any spiritual view of life. The lesson should have been learnt, and ought not to have to be repeated. Debatable issues should be treated with a finer mutual respect between scientists and theologians than in the regrettable nineteenth century.'[1]

It is certainly true that science and religion do not now fight over the same ground as they did even as recently as the nineteenth century; but it does not, I think, follow that the battle is over, at least so far as the social sciences are concerned. And it is quite certainly untrue that the present boundaries between the two combatants are the result of a belated recognition by both parties that there never was really anything to fight about. Those boundaries are simply the outcome of the continuous defeat of religion and the victorious advance of science, particularly natural science. If the natural sciences are no longer in conflict with religion, it is because religion no longer dares to say anything about the behaviour of natural phenomena, having always been proved wrong when it did so. The sun does not go round the earth, the Bible story of the creation is not true, you are more likely to avoid smallpox by vaccination than by prayer. There are, indeed, a few lingering survivals: prayers for rain are, for instance, still offered in the churches during periods of drought; but these probably survive only because science has not yet found any reliable way of turning on rain when it is wanted. In the absence of any effective alternative, the ineffectiveness of the prayers can more easily pass unnoticed.

These retreats have now gone so far that a Bishop of the Church

---

[1] *How Came Our Faith?* by W. H. L. Elmslie (Cambridge University Press), p. 86.

of England can openly disavow the central miracles of the Gospel story, though with consequences to himself and the Church which are not yet fully disclosed. Modern man, 'with his thought shaped by scientific investigation, is certain that miracles, in the sense of finite scale activities contrary to the normal ordering of nature, do not happen.'[1] According to Dr. Barnes, belief even in the story of the resurrection has to be 'abandoned'[1] for 'we cannot, out of deference to religious sentiment, reject the principle of the uniformity of nature which is fundamental in the outlook created by modern science'.[1] Only one small corner remains, somewhat precariously preserved by the Eddington-Jeans flirtations with indeterminacy, in which direct divine intervention in physical events may still be conceivable for the Bishop. 'It remains possible, and even most probable, that creative activity which the Christian would ascribe to God, may be taking place continuously ; but such activity must be in the realm of extremely small particles, such as the genes in the living cell'.[2]

This withdrawal of religion into a distinctively spiritual sphere involves certain risks to the vividness and personal quality of religious life. Any relationship with a deity who never interferes in the ordinary visible events of daily life at all, leaving these entirely to the impersonal laws of science, must clearly be different from the relation that can be made with a God who will directly respond, for instance, to prayers for our own or our friends' recovery from illness. In a sense the contact is less personal : certainly it is more restricted. The relationship between personal beings to which we are accustomed by our human experience is both physical and emotional. We go about and do things with and for our friends : we also love them. If in the course of friendship we could not interfere in the physical events of daily life, if we could not write to our friends, or visit them, or give and receive presents from them, our relationship would certainly be changed, and most of us would feel that it was impoverished. In

---

[1] *The Rise of Christianity* by Ernest William Barnes, Bishop of Birmingham (Longmans), pp. 66, 164.
[2] *Ibid*, p. 66.

the cruder, anthropomorphic forms of religion which science has now undermined, this dual relationship existed between man and God. Now the one half of it has been destroyed, and some may well feel that in this case also the result is impoverishment. Certainly, the modern form of religion which frankly admits this remoteness of God from the physical order is likely to lead to loss of faith amongst the multitude. It is at least easier to ignore a God who will in no case interfere with the physical events which necessarily occupy so much of our time and attention on earth, who did not in any direct literal sense create us, and who does not order the sun and moon in their paths. Unquestionably, by thus limiting the sphere of God's activities, science has been responsible for the decline of popular religious belief.

These losses are not, however, irreparable, and they may even be represented as gains, so long as religion is only driven out of the territory now occupied by the *natural* sciences. If God does not intervene in the physical order, relationship with him becomes exclusively spiritual. And that, the religious may argue, is all to the good. It may be more effective to take M and B than to pray to God to cure you of your pneumonia : but by prayer you may still derive strength to bear your illness cheerfully, to use it to give you sympathy with the sufferings of others, and to bring you into closer spiritual relationship with God. Anyhow, you can get into personal touch with God about this and other matters, confident still that if they are of concern to you, they are of concern to him also. It is true that such a purely spiritual relationship is probably more difficult of attainment, and certainly less often attained, than the relation postulated by the old anthropomorphic picture of God, so that there is still the risk that unbelief will become more widespread. Even that, however, may be represented as a long-term gain; since a crudely anthropomorphic religion may be judged hardly worth having, and there may be hope that in time the perceptions of those who are now spiritually blind may be wakened.

Fresh dangers, however, appear when the social sciences join with the natural sciences to explain the phenomena of consciousness, of religious experience and even of morals. That is why it is premature to speak of the battles of science and religion as having come to an end.

> ... 'the present apparent lull in the conflict between science and religion is exceedingly deceptive. Science has largely dislodged religion from its front line of trenches. The old view of the structure of the universe is universally given up. At present what is happening is that psychologists are hauling up their guns into position with a view to an assault on the second line, namely, religious psychology'.[1]

Religion could indeed retreat, without catastrophic loss, before the advance of the natural sciences, since this did not disturb its occupation of the whole field of human experience and relations. But the advance of science, and particularly of the social sciences, into this territory contains a new and still more alarming threat; because if this province is lost, there will be precious little left at all. Since the social sciences are only in their infancy, the threat is only just beginning to take shape; but there is little doubt that as it develops with the progress of these sciences, there will again be fierce battles, of which only the first skirmishes have yet been seen. The physical and human sciences between them have already begun to establish laws of association between physical events in the brain and mental experiences: there is at least a risk that in time they will find that the religious experiences now accepted as communion with God may also be associated with purely human events, mental or physical, and explicable therefore on an entirely godless hypothesis. Further, brain surgery can already profoundly modify personality and patterns of behaviour; and psychiatry has begun to account for moral conviction in terms which make any deity superfluous. The psychologists and physiologists cannot, in fact, be trusted to obey Canon Richardson's instruction to keep out. A student of Freudian theories of delinquency whom I once heard sadly remark: 'there is no more sin, there is only the cruel stepmother', may well have been a portent of bitter struggles that are to come. For the Christians have cause to remember that every

---

[1] *The Inequality of Man and Other Essays* by J. B. S. Haldane, F.R.S. (Pelican Books), p. 132.

time that the physical sciences have provided purely natural explanations of phenomena hitherto accounted for in supernatural terms, the natural explanation has eventually prevailed ; and they have reason, therefore, to fear that the same thing will happen with the intrusion of scientific method into the world of human experience and behaviour.

In that case it is, of course, *possible* to retreat again : to argue that just as God controls the behaviour of atoms and of physical objects indirectly through the laws of physics, or the state of our health indirectly through the laws of physiology and chemistry, instead of by direct personal manipulation, so also he controls our mental processes no less indirectly through the laws of physiology and psychology, including those that govern the operations of the unconscious mind. Similarly, in the field of morals, it is *possible* to argue that specific rules such as the injunction not to commit adultery, or to keep holy the Sabbath day are purely provisional interpretations of some more profound and far-reaching principle which is itself the subject of progressive revelation. There are, indeed, signs that some of the more perspicacious minds in the Churches have already begun to avail themselves of this line of retreat : repeating, in fact, exactly the story of their withdrawal from the territory claimed by the natural sciences, with this difference only, that on this occasion they are getting away without waiting to put up a fight. Thus, in the Committee recently appointed by the Archbishop of Canterbury to enquire into the problems raised by artificial insemination, the Dean of St. Paul's differed from his colleagues in that he did not feel able to condemn insemination of a woman by anyone other than her husband as necessarily contrary to Christian principles.[1] Even the Christian teaching on the family and on the sin of adultery, in his view, though not in that of the majority of the Committee, must be regarded as merely the provisional expression of the duty of Christians to love one another, which alone is unqualified and universally binding.[1]

---

[1] *Artificial Human Insemination*. Report of a Commission appointed by His Grace the Archbishop of Canterbury (S.P.C.K.) : Note by the Dean of St. Paul's, pp. 59 ff.

The dangers of this road of escape should, however, be obvious. For a God who leaves not only physical occurrences, but also mental and spiritual and moral experiences, to the mercy of impersonal and unchanging laws of association becomes extraordinarily remote and unsatisfying. It would be difficult to keep up friendship, much more to feel passionate devotion, towards anyone whose sole response on all occasions was: 'I am sorry, but I cannot do anything about it: the matter is now outside my control'. It must be hardly less difficult to worship or to love a God, who, having invented the laws of psychology and physiology, leaves suffering humanity to make the best of the consequences. Indeed, as first physical, then mental, emotional and even spiritual events become more and more clearly governed by laws of association between empirical phenomena, and therefore less and less occasion for the direct intervention of the deity, we get nearer and nearer to the point at which the difference between a religious and a secular interpretation of the universe becomes negligible.

In the last resort, the theologian and the agnostic, the convinced atheist and the Christian, are all alike faced with the fact that a world of empirical phenomena, apparently governed throughout by laws of association, presents itself to their senses. The agnostic and the atheist are unable to account for its existence: it is there, they say, it works according to the rules of science, and that is all that we know. If the deist, for his part, likes to call it the creation of God, and to see these rules as a progressive revelation of the divine mind, that comes to much the same thing, once it is admitted that this God keeps his hands completely off his own creation. The agnostic or the atheist might prefer to call this God 'unknown first principle' or 'x', or to give him some other equally impersonal title: but the difference becomes merely one of nomenclature once the supposedly direct personal relationship between God and his creatures has been shown to be as capable of a purely natural explanation as is the relation between smallpox and vaccination. 'What I must not do', writes Professor Herbert

SCIENCE AND METAPHYSICS

Butterfield, clearly sensing the dangers already, 'is to make God less than a person—hanging as a shapeless vapour or undifferentiated ooze, which is what some people seem to arrive at when they want to believe in God without committing themselves to anything.'[1] There could, indeed, hardly be a better name than 'shapeless and undifferentiated ooze' for the state to which the combined achievements of the natural and the social sciences threaten to reduce the deity who was once so active and intimate a participant in the events of our daily lives.

Nevertheless, up till now a number of professional students of the social sciences have retained a religious and sometimes even a specifically Christian faith. They have had to throw away a lot of bath water, but have succeeding in persuading themselves that at least some sort of a baby has, by various compromises, been retained. No compromise, however, can conceal the fundamental dilemma that the more specific the faith or doctrine, the more vulnerable it is to the advance of science; or that, conversely, surrender on specific points leads by an inevitable gradualness to the dissolution of anything that is worth calling a religion at all. Certainly, in my experience, many students who have been brought up in a Christian or other specifically religious faith, and who turn to the study of the social sciences, reach a point at which they are troubled by the difficulty of reconciling their religion and their scientific studies. Sometimes at this stage they give up their sociological enquiries, unable to 'follow the argument whithersoever it leads': sometimes they accept one or other of the current compromises, throwing away as much of the specific content of their religion as they dare; and sometimes their religious faith surrenders completely to the relentless encroachments of science. But whatever the outcome, the conflict that they glimpse at the moment of crisis is profoundly real. Whatever subsequent adjustment each may personally make, the incompatibility of the uninhibited pursuit of science and of faith in something more personal than an 'undifferentiated ooze' remains. Meantime deep

---
[1] in *The Listener*, 12th May, 1949, p, 796.

and unnecessary misery is inflicted on all who, because they have been taught from childhood to accept as sacred fact what is merely somebody's guess, grow up afraid to discard their religious swaddling clothes.

Finally, we must note that a religious view of the universe is in the last resort essentially anthropocentric: religion has no significance unless God cares not only for the whole human race, but for each individual human soul. Yet nothing that science has discovered, to put the matter at its lowest, gives support to the view that the Creator attaches so much importance to this particular part of his handiwork. The minute fraction of the universe on which the human drama is staged, the probably brief duration of the whole human episode, and the close connection between the mental and moral structure of a personality and the physical condition of the shortlived body with which it is associated—all this weighs heavily in the scales against the anthropocentric interpretation of the universe implied by faith in the reality of communion with a personal deity.

The doctrine that faith and science can live happily side by side, each cultivating its own garden of experience, must in the end therefore be cold comfort to the religious. For the social sciences will no more keep to their side of the fence in the twentieth century than did the natural sciences in the nineteenth; and their conquests may well be equally sweeping. In this there is, however, cause not for regret, but for rejoicing. The various superstitions, not excepting Christianity, which have passed under the name of religion, have a melancholy record of cruelty and intolerance. Of that record the best of their adherents are, indeed, now ashamed. But hardly less lamentable are the shackles which they have placed on the freedom of the human mind to follow every argument whithersoever it leads, the confusion which they have created between dogma, hypothesis and scientific law—not only in the fields of religion—and, not least, their arrogant assumption of the right to dictate in the field of morals.

CHAPTER SIX

SCIENCE AND MORALS

I

'IT must never be forgotten,' writes Dr. Norman Campbell[1], 'that, though science helps us in controlling the external world, it does not give us the smallest indication in what direction that control should be exercised ... Since science must always exclude from its province judgments concerning which differences are irreconcilable, it can only guide practical life in the choice of means, and not in the choice of ends.' A similar limitation is set by Professor George Lundberg, one of the strongest advocates of the potentialities of social science, when he writes that 'no science tells us what to do with the knowledge that constitutes the science ... There is nothing in either physical or social science which answers this question'.[2] In other words, science cannot discriminate between moral and immoral ends or between different codes of morality. Science establishes laws of association, but laws of association are like maps: they show you which road leads to which destination, but they cannot tell you where you ought to go. So there comes a point, in questions of morals, or, indeed, in any choice of ultimate ends, at which science can no longer speak with authority.

This much, indeed, we are bound at some point to admit, though it does not follow that science has no hints to give on the matter, still less that she has no comment to make on the authoritarian judgments made by others. Nor is it quite so clear as the statements just quoted would suggest, where the point lies at

---
[1] *What is Science?* pp. 160, 162.
[2] *Can Science Save Us?* by George A. Lundberg (Longmans), p. 31.

which science must abdicate. Both Dr. Campbell and Professor Lundberg, it will be noticed, ignore any problem about where means end and ends begin. In practice, however, this is not such a simple matter to determine; and the possibilities of the application of scientific method to social problems depends in large measure upon where this critical line is drawn. Dr. Campbell does not himself have anything further to say on the subject except to remark that we may be dishonest (or just muddled) about it, attempts often being made to pass off ends as means. In 'controversial matters there is always a tendency to conceal questions of ends and to pretend that every question is one of means only'—as for instance in politics, where it is 'claptrap to announce portentously that we all desire the welfare of the community and to pretend that we differ only in our view of the best way of attaining it; what we really differ about is our ideas of the welfare of the community . . .'[1]

If it is true that science cannot determine the choice of ends, it is, of course, equally true that we cannot look to science to decide what is an end and what only a means: because that decision is itself a choice of ends. If, for example, we say that we ought to be kind so that other people will like us, popularity is evidently the end that we have chosen, and kindness is only the means to it: if, alternatively, we say that we must be kind because it is good to be kind, kindness is an end in itself. Nor is there any scientific way of determining which of these ends is to be preferred either morally or on any other ground, except in terms of some given criterion; though, as is suggested below,[2] certain attitudes on moral issues may be more in harmony than others with a scientific outlook.

There are, however, three comments that are relevant at this stage to the problem of drawing the line between ends and means. In the first place, the further back the line between ends and means is drawn, the larger is the field of usefulness open to the social sciences. By 'further back' I mean, in effect, 'in more general

[1] *Op. cit.* pp. 161, 162.
[2] See pp. 134 ff.

terms'. Thus, for example, if in the field of industry trade union membership is classified as an end that is good in itself, then scientific investigation must be confined to examining the means by which as many workers as possible may be induced to join trade unions. If, alternatively, trade unions are classified as one possible means towards a further end, defined perhaps as the improvement of standards of living, then the objective methods of science can be used to determine the larger question of how far, in any given case, the structure and policies of unions are likely to achieve this result.

The second point to be noticed (and it is a very old one) is that actually many of the apparent needs of everyday life are in fact means, dressed up as ends as a matter of practical convenience : they are logically derived from some much more general principle, which for practical purposes it is assumed that they will promote. Conscription, for instance, may be treated as a political end ; but, in fact, those who advocate its enactment do so because they believe that it trains the young to be manly, or that it is an important safeguard against foreign domination or for some similar reason. The ends which command approval are manliness or national independence, not the actual conscription itself; and even these may not be final, but may be in turn derived from some more general principle in the background, such as a conception of human dignity.

The confusion of means and ends does not, therefore, always take the form that Dr. Campbell suggests of 'pretending that every question is one of means only'. On the contrary there is an equally strong disposition to pass off means as ends. Socialism, for instance, is widely acclaimed as a social and political end. As we have already seen, socialism is not a term with any clearly established meaning ; but there is little doubt that the nationalisation of the means of production, distribution and exchange is, or was at one time, a cornerstone of socialist doctrine. Yet no intelligent student of politics would regard such nationalisation as a moral imperative in its own right ; it is to be advocated only as a means towards other ends, such as productive efficiency, improved status for industrial workers or fairer distribution—each of which in turn is probably derived from some still remoter end.

This habit of treating means as ends is generally due to an economy of thought, which may be either a legitimate concession to the exigencies of daily life, or a lamentable intellectual confusion. It is legitimate, in so far as life is too short to explain fully on every occasion all the reasons why we want to achieve some practical object: it is illegitimate, if it allows us to become so wedded to the means-turned-end that we refuse to look at evidence that casts doubt upon its effectiveness as a means towards the ultimate end that we have in view.

In the third place it is interesting that, at least in the field of personal morals, the tendency of more complex civilisations is to move the line between means and ends outwards. The moral codes of relatively primitive societies generally tend to regulate large tracts of conduct, often with great minuteness; and such peoples do not ordinarily feel the obligation to justify specific imperatives in terms of any more general end. In the modern industrial world, some religious bodies do, indeed, lay down fairly detailed moral codes; the Christian churches, in particular, prescribe a catalogue of sins, the content of which varies in the different communions. In a sense these specific prohibitions may be regarded as means to the overriding end, which is to carry out the will of God; but in so far as God's will on particular issues is only known by direct revelation and not by scientific inference, such commandments as 'thou shalt not commit adultery' must for practical purposes be regarded as ends in themselves. Nevertheless, even in the Christian churches there is some tendency to minimise specific injunctions and to derive the rules of moral conduct in particular instances from a general principle of Christian love. We have already noticed an example of this—though an unusual one—in the attitude adopted by the Dean of St. Paul's to the Christian teaching about marriage and the family.[1]

---

[1] See p. 115.

Where complex societies do construct elaborate codes, backed either by legal or by moral sanctions, these are generally recognised as means to an end, and are normally concerned with acts that are held to be socially obnoxious. Thus you must not drive a motor car when you are drunk : indeed, there are a great many things that you must not do with a motor car ; and you must not try to get more than your share of rationed articles. Whether well or ill-designed for their purpose, such prohibitions are plainly intended to give expression to the moral principle that every individual must show consideration for the safety and needs of his neighbours.

This discussion about the relation of means to ends has, perhaps, a somewhat abstract academic flavour. I have, however, given some attention to it, because in practice it is quite fundamental if only because it marks the limit of human co-operation. You can work with anybody whose ultimate ends coincide with your own, even if you do not see eye to eye about means, for these differences can, potentially at any rate, be scientifically resolved. But no one can drive a cart in which the horses are being urged in opposite directions. The general statement that science can 'guide the choice of means but not the choice of ends' is much too facile, unless we have a clear idea of which is which ; and in practice it is easy to be confused on the subject, both because there are temptations to dishonesty and also from failure to think clearly. The choice of social goals is moreover a happy hunting-ground for the familiar psychological process of rationalisation. We may support conscription ostensibly because it encourages the virtue of manliness, but actually because, having suffered much in the course of military service ourselves, we have an unconscious desire to inflict the same misery upon others.

In all this there is a valuable field for scientific research. We need to know what in fact is the point at which the social ends of flesh-and-blood individuals or groups of individuals begin ; how far the means which they use are objectively appropriate to their ends ; and what is the content of these ends. All these topics are open to observation and induction ; and in the course of their exploration we may succeed in the important task of pushing back ends to the place where they logically belong—which is probably very far back indeed. In this way the territory open to science may be found to be more extensive than it appears at first sight, and the prospects of fruitful cultivation correspondingly greater.

II

At some point, however, we reach an ultimate end or value which cannot be explained in terms of anything else. When Messrs. Friend and Feibleman write that 'value judgments do not have to be regarded as unanalysable and as merely normative', and that 'the fact that social relations are themselves values does not mean that as values they cannot be scientifically treated',[1] what they say is strictly true, but only in the sense that it may be possible to establish laws of association between different aspects of human behaviour, including moral judgments or codes. But the words 'merely normative' dismiss very light-heartedly a very large subject. Nor does it help much for the same authors to tell us that 'the final ideal' of the 'scientific understanding of value' is 'the mathematical measurement of all values'.[2] Values cannot, of course, be mathematically measured except in terms of other values, which must themselves be immeasurable.

At this point the accepted proofs of scientific demonstration are no longer available. In the natural sciences, proof is finally established by appeal to primitive sensory data (and in the social sciences occasionally by appeal to direct emotional experience). The characteristics of these two criteria are, as has been pointed out in Chapter II, twofold. They are practically universal and they are inevitable. If your eyes are open, you cannot help seeing : everybody whose eyes are undamaged has the experience of sight, and everybody understands what it means to feel happy or

---

[1] *What Science Really Means* by Julius W. Friend and James Feibleman (George Allen & Unwin), p. 204.
[2] *The Unlimited Community* (George Allen & Unwin), p. 311.

depressed. And these experiences are common to all mankind, irrespective of age or sex or race or level of civilisation. Whatever each may think about it, the kettle on the fire boils alike for the primitive and the sophisticated, for white and black, for young and old.

With the best will in the world we cannot find a similar standard of direct, primary, universally recognised experience which determines our notions of morality so clearly that nobody, unless perhaps a professional philosopher, worries about their validity. Sociologists have, indeed, devoted much research to answering the question whether there are any moral values that are universally held to be good by all men at all times. The first result of these researches is always to reveal the great variety of actions which are classed as moral in different human societies. In our own country it is acknowledged to be immoral to kill anybody except the enemy in time of war, or (and on this there is a considerable difference of opinion) a person who has himself been convicted of murder. Among some primitive peoples killing the very old or the very young is regarded as entirely moral, and what has come to be known as ritual murder is an expression of the highest morality. Similarly, there is the widest variety in sexual morals : monogamy, polygamy, lifelong marriage, marriage terminable at will, pre-marital unchastity, homosexual intercourse are, or have been, all morally approved by the standards of some communities in which they are practised.

Sociologists also observe that, while every human group recognises certain moral codes or moral principles, which prescribe what is or is not to be done and so embody the moral ends of that particular community, there are always individuals who deviate in greater or less degree from the prescribed path. Such people must clearly either be indifferent to moral considerations, or have private moral codes of their own.

These facts can be interpreted in either of two ways. On the one hand, it can be said that the final ends of action are simply a matter of personal preference, and that there is no meaning in words like 'good' or 'bad' and no significance in morality. What are called moral actions are those which happen to be favoured by particular groups or by particular individuals. The conformity of individuals in a particular community to a common pattern is then explained by reasons of convenience or by the psychological discomfort of being very different from other people; whilst the fact that there are always individual deviants shows that a strong-minded (or weak-willed) individual can substitute purely personal choices of his own for those favoured by the community in which he lives.

On this interpretation there is, of course, nothing more to be said except to admit that it cannot be finally refuted either by science or by logic. If I say that war is bad because of the misery it causes, and you reply that you see no harm in misery, the discussion must come to an end, since neither of us can be proved wrong except in terms of some further moral standard which either of us may reject. And the deadlock is equally final even if I base my statement on a religious foundation. For to my assertion that it is an offence against the will of God to cause misery, you can perfectly well reply that you do not believe either in God or in the validity of the revelation by which I claim to be made aware of his existence.

I shall not pursue this interpretation further because obviously there is no purpose in discussing moral problems, or the relation of science to morals, if morality has no meaning; though even from this angle it will still be possible for scientific investigation to throw light on why particular groups or individuals make the choices that they do. Such investigation, however, clearly cannot touch the essentially moral question as to which of a number of possible lines of conduct is to be regarded as morally preferable.

The alternative interpretation of the variety of actual moral systems is that all the codes of groups and individuals are 'after something'; that there is a standard, or standards, in some degree objective, which can be applied to them all, and of which they all have at least a dim apprehension. Encouragement is given to this view by the fact that there are certain subjects to which moral rules of some kind or other appear to be applied in all the human communities of which we have knowledge, though there is, as has been said, no uniformity in the actual rules themselves. For example, however diverse the content of the relevant codes may be, wholly promiscuous sexual intercourse and wholly promiscuous killing appear to be always regarded as immoral. Further, human societies perhaps differ more—though it would be unwise to stake too much on this generalisation—in their conception of the range of persons who must be treated kindly than in their estimates of the status of kindness as a virtue. For many primitive peoples, for instance, what the sociologist calls the 'in-group' consists of a relatively small tribal community, whereas the Christian is taught, in theory at least, to treat all men as brothers and even to show kindness to animals. Everywhere, however, some in-group is recognised, the members of which it is our duty to treat considerately.

From this angle differences in moral codes are explained as due not so much to 'disagreement about fundamental moral principles' as partly to 'differences in the circumstances of different societies' and partly to the 'different views which people hold, not on moral questions but on questions of fact'.[1] Sir David Ross, from whose book these quotations are taken, cites in support of this point of view the fact[2] that the approval of the blood feud in some societies and its rejection in others may be accounted for on the ground that in very primitive conditions 'where there is no proper provision for the public punishment of murderers, private vengeance is the only way of securing respect for life'. So also 'the difference between those who think vaccination right and those who think it wrong turns largely on a difference of opinion on the question of fact whether vaccination does or does not prevent smallpox, while both parties accept the principle that parents should try to save their children from disease.' Sir David, however,

---

[1] *Foundations of Ethics* by Sir W. David Ross (Clarendon Press), p. 18.
[2] Quoted by Sir David Ross from Professor Taylor in *Mind* xxxv (1926), p. 289.

leaps over rather a large chasm when he proceeds confidently to step from the proposition that 'we do not seriously question that we are nearer the truth about the physical universe than were the Greeks' to the conclusion that 'we need not doubt that man progresses fairly steadily towards moral truth as he does towards scientific'.[1] Such a jump overlooks the difference between moral and scientific truth, for moral truth is not, of course, demonstrable to the senses as are the truths of science; and if its validity is to be judged by the 'moral intuitions' which are sometimes supposed to correspond in this sphere to the senses in the world of physical phenomena, the answers will be extremely discordant.

The fact is, of course, that the firm progress which we have seen to be characteristic of strictly scientific enquiry is contingent on the establishment of some objective criterion by which truth can be distinguished from error. Sir David's confidence would be solidly founded if we could demonstrate that moral truth is contained in, say, the teachings of Jesus, or in the doctrine that moral actions are those which promote the greatest happiness of the greatest number, in the same way that we can demonstrate that water turns to steam at a given temperature. Failing such a criterion, we must, however, treat propositions about moral values or moral truths strictly as hypotheses that cannot yet be confirmed by the empirical checks that are necessary if the validity of a scientific law of association is to be finally established.

On the other hand, it does not follow that all possible hypotheses on the subject are equally consonant with the general direction of the teachings of science. Here again, as in metaphysics, we have to choose between doctrines which are derived from religious revelation, general or special, and those hypotheses which do not require any supernatural support, but are built only upon natural phenomena. Since one of the most alarming arguments commonly brought against a strictly secular approach to social and moral problems is that morals without religion are founded upon sand, it is worth while giving some attention to the nature of

---

[1] *Foundations of Ethics*, p. 20.

both religious and secular morality, and to the security or insecurity of their respective foundations.

A system of morals which is derived from the will of God obviously implies that morality is something more than what Alex Comfort has so happily called 'a private joke of the human species'.[1] Standards of right and wrong, according to this view, are objective realities inherent in the mind of God and in the nature of the universe which he has created. Our knowledge of them may still be imperfect, though increasing, perhaps, through progressive revelation; but the standards themselves are, it is implied, quite literally superhuman, and not just high-sounding names which we have invented for what are, after all, simply matters of personal preference. The truth that it is wrong to steal would thus rank with the truth that two and two make four. From the first of these lessons, just as much as from the second, the child is supposed to learn about the nature of things; and in neither case may it be said that he is just being conditioned to habits that suit the convenience of his elders, or satisfy their lust for domination.

Further, moral codes or principles which claim divine authority can invoke sanctions that are not available to their purely secular counterpart. This distinction is much in the minds of those who fear that a decline in religious belief will necessarily undermine morality. Reasons are given later for thinking that this fear is greatly exaggerated.[2] Here, however, it is relevant to notice that the sanctions of religious morality may be of two kinds. There is first the sanction which is purely spiritual: the punishment for sin is the alienation from God which it necessarily involves. But there may also be a second punishment of a different nature. Before science had limited the scope of divine interference in everyday life as severely as it has today, such punishments were supposed to take very concrete practical forms: the sinner was overtaken by illness or other worldly disaster. However, in a world where the

---

[1] *The Standard of Humanity*. (*The Listener*, 9th December, 1948, p. 882.)
[2] See pp. 154 ff.

righteous so often suffer grievously and the wicked flourish like a green bay tree, it was inevitable that such doctrines should be eventually shaken.

There remains, of course, the next world. The physical torments of hell must have been a powerful threat to those who believed in them; but with the decline of the anthropomorphic conception of an angry and cruel God, Dante's picture is discarded; or, alternatively, as I have heard it put from the angle of one Christian church, 'we have to believe in hell but we do not have to believe that anybody goes there.' The rewards and punishments of the next world therefore, like those on earth, assume an increasingly spiritual character. Nevertheless, so long as we have a vivid and confident apprehension of the reality of life after death, the prospect that one way or another the sins or the virtues of this life may affect our experiences in the next gives a sanction to morality obviously denied to those who believe that the physical death of the body means the final extinction of the whole personality.

None of these sanctions, however, is quite as solid as the churches would like to make them appear; nor are they so greatly superior to those on which secular morality must rely. The substitution of purely spiritual rewards or punishments for the crude physical notions now discarded is in danger of reducing the foundations of morality to the same kind of 'undifferentiated ooze' as that into which the deity himself already threatens to dissolve; or, to put the matter more accurately, just as the spiritual evidence for God's existence can only be appreciated by those who have eyes to see, so also a purely spiritual sanction for morality will only be effective with those who are already in a sufficient state of grace to feel suffering if they are alienated from God. The really sinful will be quite indifferent to this prospect. This is a serious difficulty, for it means that religious sanctions against immoral conduct are futile in the case of those who need them most. We are, in fact, back in the old dilemma. If the churches teach that God's anger and his love are demonstrated in concrete and practical forms in our daily lives, that is something which we can all understand, and of which, if it were true, we should all do well to take notice; but, unfortunately science has shown that it is not true. If, alternatively, God only makes his will known in spiritual terms which are plainly unintelligible to many, perhaps even to the majority, then the wicked can safely go on their way rejoicing.

In other words, if there is *any* truth in the view that standards of morality have declined with the decay of religious belief, the action of the churches themselves is largely responsible, though no doubt they could hardly have acted otherwise than they did. For it is pertinent to ask, belief in *what* has declined? If we mean belief in an anthropomorphic God who squares accounts in a thoroughly practical way, that has already been surrendered to the conquests of science. And nothing that is likely to be so widely effective remains to take its place. A morality whose sanctions can only help the spiritually-minded to be good is not built on very solid rock.

Further, the sanctions of religious systems of morality are neither better nor worse founded than the religion from which they are derived. Such systems share, therefore, the characteristics which we have found to be inherent in all theistic interpretations of the universe. By giving divine sanction to standards of human behaviour they necessarily imply the anthropocentric view of the universe implied in those interpretations; and they are accordingly open to all the objections to anthropocentrism to which reference has already been made.[1] And similarly, since religious morals rest upon faith, they, too, imply the equal validity of two distinct kinds of truth—one derived from science, and one from revelation, although the former alone is based upon primary perceptions which are at once universal, irresistible and identical for all observers.

Dependence on faith thus gives to religious morality a security which by definition lasts only so long as does the conviction behind it. There is a sense, of course, in which this is true of all

---

[1] See p. 118.

moral systems. But the peculiarity of religious systems is that this threat to security has a peculiar all-or-nothing character. To the believer, the loss of religious faith means the loss of all his moral imperatives. The agnostic moralist, on the contrary, has, as we shall see, no similar catastrophe to fear : indeed, if he is a thoughtful person, he has probably revised his moral categories more than once, without in any way weakening the practical force behind them. In the concrete terms of our own day and generation, this really means that Christian morality as everyman's working guide to the moral choices of ordinary life is founded upon sand. To the great majority of the population, who are naturally unacquainted with the dilution of Christian doctrine now taking place in the books of the theologians, Christian morality implies belief in the story that the God who created the universe at a given date caused his divine son to become incarnate in human form, and to be born of a virgin ; and that, after a life of preaching and miracles ending in death on the cross, this God-in-man rose from the dead and appeared in bodily form to his disciples. It does seem extraordinarily dangerous for any community—and particularly one which is accustomed to scientific habits of thought—to tie its everyday moral standards to belief in such an astonishing story. The sophisticated Christian may reply that this story is to be regarded as only religious symbolism, not literal truth ; but in that case it is inexplicable why it is not so presented in the versions of Christianity commonly offered to the public at large.

The dangers are, moreover, enhanced by the fact that religious morality deals in absolutes ; and yet these absolutes have themselves a way of collapsing in the face of new circumstances and new knowledge. In the course of the history of Christianity alone, it thus appears that God has enjoined the horrors of the Inquisition and forbidden the divorce and remarriage of married couples. These dictates are, however, revised from time to time, so that in ethics as well as in metaphysics we have the spectacle of doctrine which claims divine authority being steadily withdrawn from the particular to the general, each stopping-point in turn having the status of absolute divine sanction. If the God who once made the sun go round the earth is now a vague presence in the background of a universe regulated by scientific laws with which he no longer interferes, so also the God who orders the rich man to give up all for his religion now takes a liberal view of contemporary economics. Each of these retreats, however, involving as it does the surrender of a previously final position, threatens the fundamental security of religious morals, and provokes the unbeliever to ask 'why stop here?'

It would seem, therefore, that religious morality in general, and Christian morals in particular, are neither particularly well founded, nor easily brought into harmony with the picture of the universe suggested by science. But whether or no the lessons of science can be squared with the teachings of religion, there is one attitude on the subject from which every scientist must feel himself debarred. That is the attitude which urges that, since the will of God is a more powerful imperative to moral action than the uncertain judgment of man, religious myths should be upheld and preached by those who are themselves intellectually unconvinced by them. In its worst form, this policy implies the cynical opinion that other people will not be good unless they are told lies. I have personally heard this opinion (though naturally not in those words) advanced by agnostic parents as a reason for sending their children to church,[1] by agnostic schoolmasters as a reason for themselves giving religious instruction to their pupils, and by agnostic thinkers on public affairs as a reason for supporting the efforts of religious bodies to win adherents amongst the public at large. Yet, intellectual integrity is the essential condition for every step in scientific knowledge from the earliest beginnings down to the latest refinements of physics. The scientist who presents to others as fact what he himself believes to be either false or unproven betrays that integrity. Certainly, we can say straightaway that no

---

[1] This is not, of course, to deny that there may be other honest reasons why the children of agnostics should be encouraged to go to church, e.g., so that they may hear both sides of a question, or so that they may be acquainted with the dominant religious beliefs of the community in which they live.

system of morals which does not include intellectual integrity as a fundamental virtue is compatible with science.

III

If morality is neither a matter of personal preference nor derived from divine revelation, we have next to ask whether empirical observation gives any clue as to the reality of objective moral standards; and whether, in particular, some conceptions of morality are more in harmony than others with the general picture of the universe and of man himself that is presented by science. Here it is natural to look first to biology, as the science concerned with living creatures, of which man is one species; and it will, I think, be found that biological considerations both set limits to the range of choice of possible moral systems, and suggest that certain solutions to the problem are more consistent than others with the scientific approach to social questions.

The most obvious biological limitation on purely natural systems of morals is that none is workable which leads to the extermination of our species. Such a limitation does not necessarily apply to a morality which has a religious basis. Human life could be so vile in the eyes of God that he might find the universe a better place without it. There have been religions, including some versions of Christianity, which have come near to this depressing view of our earthly state: their adherents have, however, generally consoled themselves with promises of a less contemptible life after death. A purely human morality, however, which took up this position would be self-contradictory. If goodness means simply what is good *for man*, it must disappear with the disappearance of our race, and cannot, therefore, be promoted by actions which bring this about. To put the matter in another way, any moral system which is conceived in human, as distinct from supernatural, terms must contain the principle: survival is good. Possibly this is the reason why rules about killing are, as has been mentioned, characteristic of all known moral systems. If there were no such rules, the species might long ago have destroyed itself; though even this cannot be said with certainty, since many other species seem to have increased and multiplied without, so far as we know, observing any moral restraints.

Certainly, we can be quite confident that in the complex kind of social organisation which man has *now* evolved, rules on this subject have become necessary for his physical survival, as well as for (what is a different matter, though the two are often confused) the survival of our particular type of civilisation. Indeed, physical survival may well today depend not only upon *some* rules being observed, but also upon these being the right ones. Plainly this is a critical point in the construction of a viable moral system in the contemporary world. In our present precarious plight, the principle that survival is good may, in fact, lead directly to certain quite specific inferences. In particular, survival appears to have become dependent upon some at least of our moral imperatives being applied to the whole race and not merely to a limited part of it. Moral codes are, as we have already seen, often limited in their application, that is to say, they are recognised only by a particular group, and differentiate between the members of that group and those outside it—between the 'in-group' and the 'out-group'. Unless this distinction is obliterated, at least so far as the rules about killing are concerned, the actual physical survival of the race may well be gravely endangered.

This is a new situation, consequent, as everyone knows, upon the terrifying increase in our technical power; it can only be met, first, by an extension of our moral frontiers which will make these coincident with the limits of our planet; and, second, by consequential modifications in the structure of our social and political systems, since moral principles are not effective in a vacuum, but only if they are embodied in customs, laws and habits. Given, however, the moral principle that survival is good, and the further inference, derived from direct observation of the technical conditions of the contemporary world, that this principle now demands a world-wide morality, the question what precise changes in customs, habits and laws are consequently necessary, and how these may most effectively be brought about, becomes a subject for strictly scientific enquiry. It is, for instance, a commonplace that such an institution as the sovereign national state now threatens the possibility of human survival; but in view of the psychological loyalties evoked by the national state, the historical factors which have contributed to make existing states just what they are, and the many useful functions which states perform for their own nationals, only detailed empirical observation can suggest by what means and in what exact direction this institution must now be modified.

The somewhat negative proposition that scientific morality must regard actions that threaten human survival as immoral does not, happily, exhaust the hints to be derived from science about the nature of moral values. More positive suggestions are to be found in the biological concept of organism. In the words of Dr. E. S. Russell, every living organism exhibits 'a mode of activity which is shared by no inorganic object or unit and by no machine, namely, action directed towards end-states or goals which are normally related to the biological ends of self-maintenance, development or reproduction. This we may call directive activity. It can rarely be called purposive activity for the organic agent concerned is seldom explicitly aware of the goal towards which its action is directed, much less of the biological end which it subserves'.[1] Dr. Russell adds further that, if the integrity of an organism, that is to say, its achievement of its normal life-cycle of self-maintenance, development and reproduction, is disturbed, it will actively set about restoring this—it 'actively seeks out and selects the substances necessary for its metabolism, or draws them from its stores. It actively seeks in many cases its appropriate environment, and strives to maintain itself therein; it actively seeks in many cases a suitable ecological niche for its eggs and offspring. In all these ways, and in many others, the organism strives to persist in its own being, and to reach its normal completion or actualisation'.[2] Mr. Somerset Maugham quoted Fray

---
[1] *The Directiveness of Organic Activities* (Cambridge University Press), p. 3.
[2] *Ibid*, p. 190.

Luis de Leon to very nearly the same effect, though in less technical terms, when he wrote 'The beauty of life is nothing but this . . . that each should act in conformity with his nature and his business'.[1]

The essentials of this theory seem to be : first, that for every organism there exists a condition of full normal development ; second, that the specific goal towards which activity such as the healing of a wound or the maintenance of body temperatures is directed is governed by the need to achieve this condition and to reproduce offspring who in turn may achieve it ; third, that while such activity is seldom conscious, it nevertheless differs from movement in the inorganic world, inasmuch as there is 'active persistence' towards the goal, and 'use of alternative means towards the same end'. Thus the cat, whose sympathetic system has been put out of action so that it cannot make the normal psychological responses to cold, tries to keep itself warm by getting out of draughts or by shivering with exceptional violence ; whereas the stone which is rolling down the hill, if stopped by some obstacle, gives up, so to speak, the attempt to get to the bottom. Finally, while this direct yet flexible activity is mainly unconscious, 'human directiveness and purposiveness in thought and action are a specialised development of the directiveness and creativeness inherent in life'.[2]

Self-maintenance, reproduction and, in a purely physical sense, development, are as much the goals of man as of any other species, and in the human organism, as in others, their pursuit is largely an unconscious process. But over and above this, man's biological peculiarity—his mind—both enables him to superimpose conscious upon unconscious processes, and even requires that he should do so. The power which intelligence confers can be, and is, directed toward the goal of physical health, first, at a pre-scientific level by the activities of medicine-men, and later, as science advances, by modern medical practice ; and in consequence the human organism sometimes recovers from injuries and

---
[1] *The Summing Up* (Heinemann), p. 317.
[2] Russell, *op. cit.*, pp. 144, 178.

diseases which would have proved fatal to animals that could not treat them. This same power, however, itself imposes new demands. The mind has what Dr. Russell calls its own 'structuro-functional norms', and creatures that are endowed with mind as well as body have a biological need to keep this organ up to standard as much as any other. For the human species, with its highly specialised mental capacities, full normal development must therefore mean more than the realisation of physical potentialities : it must include a comparable development of the potentialities of the mind.

Ours is thus the double goal of mental and physical health. The concept of mental health which has lately come to occupy an increasingly prominent place in our thought and in our vocabularies is, I think, of great significance as giving a clue to the nature of the values that are good for man ; for man, that is, when he has come to see himself as a uniquely complex biological species, rather than as the focus of a hypothetical deity's attention. What is good for man in this sense means as for other organisms what secures his 'completion' ; but in his case this means full development of mind as well as of body. Such development of the mental and physical potentialities of human organisms may thus be the key to our ultimate moral principle, moral actions being those which promote this development : immoral ones those which obstruct it. If Sir David Ross and other philosophers are right in thinking that there is some common principle after which all the various moral codes of the world are groping, it may well be this. But whether or no we all even now dimly appreciate the goal towards which we should be striving, it is certainly true that a system of moral values conceived in terms of physical and mental health fits with peculiar aptness into the framework of science. It brings the moral activities of our uniquely endowed species into harmony with the 'directiveness and creativeness inherent' in all life ; it is consistent with the discoveries of science in the fields of biology and psychology ; and it does no violence to scientific method, since it does not require any superfluous, still less any supernatural, hypothesis. I know no other system of moral values of which all these things can be said. Nor is it, as is sometimes suggested, 'materialistic' and therefore 'degrading' to bring man's mental, including his emotional and artistic, nature under the same biological umbrella as his physical body. The biological goal of physical health can justly be labelled as 'materialistic'; but the mind, whatever its relation to the body may turn out to be, is not *the same* as the body; and the goal of mental health cannot be described as 'physical' or 'material' in the sense in which those words are normally used of the body. A system of values which is based on mental and physical health is natural in the sense that it makes no supernatural or, indeed, extra-human claims, but, by definition, it is not just a matter of flesh pots. The ideal is neither the pig satisfied nor Socrates dissatisfied: but Socrates satisfied.

Admittedly, we know as yet very little about mental health. Since we have only just begun to think in these terms, that is hardly surprising. We can, however, already say with confidence that mental health is founded upon happiness; and that it implies in addition on the emotional side, the kind of happiness that is enriched by the happiness of other people, and the harmonious social relations to which this leads; and, on the intellectual side, full development of intellectual capacity. Perfect mental health is, moreover, an active and conscious state, knowingly enjoyed by its possessors. On the negative side, the healthy mind is free both from cruelty and aggression, and from extremes of asceticism and self-abnegation.

A system of moral values that equates the human good with whatever promotes man's mental and physical health may be criticised on the ground that a mentally healthy person is an entirely subjective concept, and means nothing more than the kind of person that psychiatrists admire. There are, however, weighty arguments against such a view. First, it is significant that physical health is a goal the conscious desire for which is, as nearly as may be, universal throughout mankind: there is no other conscious aim which can match it in this respect. Sophisticated and primitive peoples alike seek to be well, although, of course, the different techniques which they employ for the purpose are by no means equally effective. A system of values which includes physical health as good commands, therefore, a universal consensus of approval almost comparable to the universal conviction of the reality of sensory experience upon which all scientific knowledge is based. Moreover, health for species other than man admittedly means the health of the whole organism, including all its parts. By analogy one would expect the same rule to apply to man. A lion is not healthy if it has an abscess on its tail. A man has no tail, but has, on the other hand, a mind such as the lion (apparently) lacks; and a man is not healthy if he has the equivalent of an abscess on his mind. In short, the grounds for accepting the objectivity of mental health are in the last resort the same as the grounds for accepting the objectivity of physical health.

Secondly, these arguments are reinforced by the close connection, demonstrated by modern medical and psychological research, between mental and physical sickness. An increasing number of bodily diseases like digestive disturbances are found to be commonly associated with mental states—a relationship which points strongly to the conclusion that health for our species is a single, not a dual, condition. That, indeed, is just what one would expect by analogy both from other creatures, and from man's own physical nature. A septic wound raises the temperature of the body, not merely of the injured limb, and the fever induces pains in parts of the body that have themselves suffered no injury. In other words, the physical health of the body must be treated as a whole, liable to be affected by what happens in any of its parts. Similarly, sickness of mind is linked with sickness of body: this connection works both ways, sickness of certain bodily organs, notably the brain, affecting the mind, and sickness of the mind in turn affecting other parts of the body. It is reasonable, therefore, to infer that just as a disease of some physical organ impairs the whole physical health of the organism, so physical and mental health are themselves also interrelated and to be treated as a unity;

the true concept of health being the complete physical-cum-mental development of the organism.

There is, therefore, good ground for thinking that the concept of mental health is neither more nor less objective than that of physical health; and that both are part of the ends of 'self-maintenance, development and reproduction', which we share with all biological species and which constitute what is 'good' for us as for any other organism.

Mental development, as a biological end, does, however, differ in important respects from its physical counterpart. In the first place, a high innate capacity for mental development (in which, of course, we must include more than the purely intellectual factors in mind) has probably little survival value. Biological adaptation in the physical sense is promoted by the close relationship between adaptive success and physical survival. The organism which cannot come to terms with its environment so as to achieve self-maintenance, development and reproduction, is exterminated. Man, however, can maintain and reproduce himself successfully at a very poor level of mental health. Some aspects of mental development—the development of the intelligence for instance—have no doubt in some circumstances a survival value. Since man's intelligence has been his most powerful weapon in the conquest of his material environment and in conflict with members of his own species, there must in the course of our history have been some selection in favour of intelligence; but intelligence is only one aspect of the mind. Mental health, as we are beginning to understand it in the sense of full intellectual and emotional development, has very little relation in any circumstances to bodily survival. Even when, as we have seen, mental sickness leads to bodily sickness, it is only in rare cases that this is sickness unto death. Indeed, since psychosomatic illnesses seem to be unconscious attempts on the part of an emotionally frustrated patient to gain attention, they are generally directed towards producing chronic or repeated illness rather than death—which would, indeed, be a disastrous failure of the mechanism!

In the second place, the mental health of any given organism cannot, to anything like the same extent as its bodily development, be taken care of by unconscious processes. It is as though in the one case nature had supplied us with a self-maintaining and self-repairing outfit; in the other case she has given us the tools (and exceptionally delicate and complex ones at that) and left us to finish the job. The biological end of mental health will not, therefore, look after itself; the unconscious maintenance or development of an organ of consciousness is very nearly, if not quite, a contradiction in terms.[1] A mind must by its own efforts try to find the path of its own development; and the whole history of mankind is evidence that it does not achieve this as surely as cut flesh heals.

Thirdly, the mental completion of any individual is far more dependent, even at primitive levels of social development, than is his physical health, upon co-operative social processes. The mind of a human organism must live in a kind of symbiotic relationship with other minds. This means that the fulfilment of our mental ends is not only a conscious, but also a social, process. The man who has achieved the completion proper to a member of his species must be fully developed in mind and body. The body will partly (but not wholly) look after itself below the level of consciousness. The mind must consciously concern itself with its own development; but it can only do this within the limits of the way of life evolved by the group of minds of which it is one member. In an elaborately organised society, the health of the body as well as that of the mind may, indeed, be critically dependent upon the behaviour of its neighbours: no resident in an industrial city can so much as feed himself. But, however close this physical dependence may become, it still does not supersede the unconscious bodily processes which continue to get on with their part of the job, digesting food, eliminating waste, healing wounds and so on.

---

[1] Perhaps in view of the phenomena of hypnosis and suggestion, it is better not to say 'quite'.

SCIENCE AND MORALS

A system of moral values, therefore, which identifies the good of the human species with the physical and mental self-maintenance, development and reproduction of its members, demands, on the mental side, both that the individual organism should consciously seek this good for itself, and that this organism should live in a good society, correspondingly defined as one which does everything possible to promote this good for all its members. And this in turn, since a society is only a group of individuals acting co-operatively and not an entity over and above them, means that every individual must contribute by his own co-operative action to the making of such a good society.

In view of the complexity of these demands, it is hardly surprising that we should in practice be so muddled about the ends of social action, so confused in our moral codes, and, indeed, so thankful to throw the whole responsibility on to the shoulders of a deity who is at least unable to complain. Nor is it surprising that the muddle should have continued so long, or that we should have barely reached the medicine-man stage in our search for mental health. Because there is no natural selection to eliminate the failures, there is no inevitability about moral, as contrasted with physical, evolution.[1] Judged by the scale of human life, physical evolution is extremely slow; but moral evolution need never happen at all. If the mind has, in common with the rest of our organism, an inherent tendency to direct action towards its own fulfilment, it has also, just because it is conscious, a peculiar capacity to fail in that direction—to misdirect, rather than to direct, activity towards the appropriate end; and every man's mind is in some degree at the mercy of its fellows.

Nevertheless, if there is no inevitability about moral evolution, it is also true that if and when we do hit upon the moral standards which are appropriate to our species, there is, thanks to scientific method, no reason at all why these should not be rapidly trans-

---

[1] As indicated in Chap. IV, some of the most insidious fallacies in sociological reasoning have resulted from failure to recognise that there is no parallel in 'social evolution' to the natural selection that operates in evolution in the strictly physical sense.

lated into the corresponding ways of behaviour. If we know what mental and physical health are, and we are clear that these are the ends that we are after, then the task of devising the social and political institutions and moral codes that make these ends possible is a practical research job for the social sciences. We can get ahead with it as soon as we have freed ourselves from the obscurantism that I have described in Chapters III and IV of this book ; and we can reasonably hope that the rewards will be comparable with those of scientific enquiry in other fields.

Systems of value which rest upon no supernatural foundation are often accused of having simply borrowed Christian morality while dispensing with the Christian sanctions : they undermine, it is said, the foundation of what is old and yet have nothing new to add. Reasons have already been given for thinking that the effectiveness of the sanctions for Christian morality has been much exaggerated : the positive sanctions that can be adduced in support of agnostic morality are discussed later.[1] But the charge of simple plagiarism cannot, I think, be substantiated. It is true that many of the Christian virtues, such as kindness and truthfulness, find a place in nearly all humanist systems of morals. But these virtues were not invented by Christianity, and Christians have no monopoly of them. They are, however, interpreted by Christians with a particular emphasis ; and there are points at which a moral system that is derived from mental and physical health, regarded as the biological ends of our species, is likely to diverge from the Christian interpretation.

Consider, for example, the relation of the self to the happiness of others. It is not easy to express precisely in words the difference between, on the one hand, the mind whose personal happiness is 'simply and naturally enriched by the happiness of others,' and, on the other hand, the mental attitude which finds in the happiness of others (or more commonly in good works or in the happiness of *an*other) a kind of compensatory satisfaction for its own frustration ; yet any psychologically observant person could

---

[1] See pp. 154 ff.

illustrate the distinction from examples within his own experience. From the angle of mental health the distinction is significant; for in the latter case there is often an element of pathological self-sacrifice. Traditional Christian morality, however, with its emphasis upon the absolute virtue of the sacrifice of self for others, has given little place to this distinction. Similarly, the asceticism which, though by no means universal in Christian teaching, has yet been so widely preached by Christians is clearly repugnant to a conception of moral welfare which requires the complete fulfilment of the potentialities of the human organism.

Further proof that the secular moralists have not simply helped themselves lock, stock and barrel to Christian morals is to be found in the different attitude which they often adopt towards the Christian teaching on sexual morality, on the one hand, and towards the rest of the Christian ethic on the other. On sexual morality a great diversity of opinion, not to say a great perplexity, prevails today amongst serious agnostic thinkers in countries which are heirs to the Christian tradition; and this diversity is reflected in the practice of the much larger numbers who are not the makers of thought on these questions. The Christian ideal of pre-nuptial chastity and monogamous marriage is demonstrably not attained; and it is violated not only by those who believe it to be right but find it too difficult to achieve, but also by many who are quite unconvinced of its inherent rightness in all circumstances. It is significant, perhaps, that this is one field in which man, in the course of his history, has tried practically every imaginable pattern—monogamy, polygamy, polyandry, lifelong marriage, marriage terminable at will and so on. Psycho-analytic research has thrown a good deal of light on the relation between sexual life and mental health or ill-health; and from this we may be able to deduce at least negative rules, and to modify existing patterns accordingly, even though firm positive knowledge is still scanty. Much, for instance, has been learned about the contribution to neurotic illness in children and adults of an emotionally unsatisfactory domestic background; and enough is known to make the extreme rigidity of the orthodox Christian pattern suspect. Conceivably, we may in the end cease to regard sexual morality as a special province, applying to it only those moral rules about kindness and consideration that relate to personal relationships generally. In the meantime, those who are accustomed to a scientific attitude will not be disturbed by uncertainty: the provisional hypothesis which markes for them the frontiers of knowledge is familiar ground, on which they do not fear to pitch their moving camp.

On the other hand, agnostics are far more ready to accept the Christian code on kindness. Cruelty or unkindness may be much commoner than adultery or fornication, yet they are much more widely felt to be wrong. The secular moralists cannot, therefore, be said to be simply stealing the Christian ethic or rechristening Christianity. Part of this ethic they accept on merits: part they explicitly reject, in an attitude of rational discrimination towards both the Christian and other moral systems.

IV

If we accept the promotion of mental and physical health as the basis of our system of values, how far does this make it possible to pass judgment upon the diverse moral codes still operative in the world? Right and wrong mean different things to the ritual murderer and to the Western colonist in Africa, to the Russian Communist and to the typical Frenchman or American of our time. To the sociologically-trained moralist, always uncomfortably aware of this diversity, this is a peculiarly baffling problem. Conceivably, he may agree that the 'normal completion or actualisation' of the human organism actually has a different meaning in different human societies; and that, while the goal itself is an objective reality in each particular case, there are, nevertheless, no standards common to the whole human race, and therefore none in terms of which the Americans can, say, pass judgment upon the Polynesians, or *vice versa*. The local and temporary character of moral codes gives some countenance to this view; but there are stronger reasons for its rejection. For in the first place, the common element in these codes, to which reference has already been made, gives at least a hint of a more general standard. Secondly, the notion that distinctive yet objective moral goals are appropriate to different human societies brings us dangerously near to the fallacies which it was the object of Chapter IV to expose. The organism whose 'actualisation and completion' it is the purpose of morality to promote is the individual human being, not the artificial, slippery entity that passes under the name of a particular human society. This organism must indeed live in some kind of organised society, because social intercourse, and in the ordinary case economic co-operation also, are necessary for its maintenance and development. Development may indeed be a process of mutual interaction; but the goals towards which the creative activity of a group is directed are realised in, and only in, the individual organisms of which that group is composed.

Thirdly, all the evidence that we possess suggests that the innate mental differences between different racial or local groups are much less marked then their similarities. Investigation into the intellectual capacities of individuals of various races (intelligence being the mental factor in which the technique of measurement has been carried furthest) is inconclusive on the subject of whether there are any differences between the average (or the extreme) levels reached by the members of different races; and the same is true also of the less precise measurements of other mental factors so far attempted. But the available evidence that we have in every case indicates that the differences between individuals within a given racial group are much larger than any divergences between racial averages. The spread from the exceptionally brilliant through the mediocre to the stupid is found in all races; and no racial group has a monopoly of the highly extroverted, or of intermediate types, or of the extreme introvert. Nor has anything as yet emerged to suggest that the native Africans, for instance, live in the various ways that they do because of their innate characters as negroes. On the contrary, their success in adapting themselves to entirely different modes of life in other parts of the world refutes any such hypothesis; and the same is true of other races.

If, then, the mental and physical goals of the human organism are in all conditions substantially the same, and if the attainment of these goals is the ultimate moral objective, it follows that the diversity of actual moral standards is to be explained in one or other of two ways. It may be due, on the one hand, to failure to understand correctly what this moral objective implies. Just as many peoples are quite ignorant of the laws of physical health, so they may be no less ignorant about moral health: unquestionably all our moral standards are to some extent defective in this sense. Alternatively, although the essential goal of the organism remains the same, the practical means by which it is best achieved may differ in differing circumstances. The kind of actions, for instance, that are necessary if we are adequately to fulfil our duty to our neighbour and assist him fully to realise the potentialities of his organism may be quite different according to whether we live in a complex industrial civilisation, or amongst American pioneers, or in a contemporary Mexican village. In the first case that duty perhaps consists largely in honest dealing with the Inland Revenue or equivalent tax-collecting departments, in the second in direct physical and emotional assistance to those who are sick or otherwise in trouble, and in the third in faithful discharge of communal tasks in cultivation. Such differences are plainly the direct consequence of the varied cultural patterns to which different human groups conform. To borrow Ruth Benedict's illuminating image, experience shows that there is a wide arc[1] of potential ways of life to which the highly adaptable innate human stuff may be conditioned. Towards the ends of this arc violence is clearly done to the normal and healthy development of the human mind; but within these limits there remains a large range of possible modes of behaviour. The circumstances which lead this community to lay

---

[1] *Patterns of Culture* (Routledge), p. 17.

emphasis on one, and that community on another, of the great variety of possible cultural patterns are extremely complex. Physical environment plays its part : life in Greenland is necessarily different from life at the Equator. Not less significant are the contacts of one culture with others : the cultural pattern of the West Indian islands, for instance, has blended together relics of the attitudes inculcated by a slave society, vestiges of African tribal beliefs heavily overlaid with several versions of Christianity, contemporary American slang and British political ideas.

Such wide cultural differences may reasonably be expected to imply corresponding differences in the practical codes of morals necessary to create conditions in which the human organism can 'persist in its own being and reach its normal completion or actualisation'. This would still be true even if we knew a great deal more than we do both about the nature of the conditions conducive to this end in different circumstances, or about the norm of mental-cum-physical health itself. In the meantime, it is impossible to say with confidence which elements in a given moral code are due to sheer misconception of the needs of the human organism, and which are due to recognition that in different cultural and physical environments those needs must be satisfied in different ways. We can, therefore, still only make limited judgments about the conflicting versions of right and wrong which have ruled men's lives in this or that continent in one age or another. We may, perhaps, be confident that where life is largely governed by fear (whether fear of the gods or of the people in power, or of anything else), mental development will be stunted. The connection between mental health and a sense of security in personal relationships is well established ; but of the relation of mental-cum-physical health, for instance, to particular norms of sexual behaviour, we know practically nothing.

As knowledge grows, however, the area over which judgment must be suspended will be diminished ; and if the full mental and physical development of all its members comes to be accepted as the goal of the species, we may expect to see less diversity in the prevailing conceptions of good and evil and the moral codes in which these are embodied. Such unification is in itself to be welcomed because people cannot live closely together, bound by common ties in work and play, unless there is a considerable consistency in their moral values. If A thinks right what B thinks wrong and both act accordingly, social organisation, that is to say, the establishment of reliable relations between people, cannot be maintained between them. Only isolated communities having strictly limited relations with one another can afford to diverge widely in their conceptions of good and evil : on this subject the polite agreement to differ is practicable only so long as it is accompanied by a polite agreement to live separately. In the contemporary world, however, isolation is for technical reasons becoming less and less possible for any human group. Here, indeed, is something of a dilemma for the anthropologists, who plead, from so many points of view laudably, against the ruthless imposition of Western modes of life upon unsophisticated native peoples, but must yet recognise that divergent *moral* values can only be preserved at the price of exclusion from the world community. For the small primitive group such isolation is, perhaps, still possible, though hardly to be desired ; but the dangers of moral divergence between large groups which have reached a high level of technical development and social organisation needs no comment in the light of this century's experience.

The unification of moral codes that would follow upon general acceptance of mental and physical development as the basis of our moral systems on the one hand, and increasing knowledge of what this goal demands on the other hand, must not be confused with a general standardisation of culture. The human species shows remarkable variability in the physical and mental make-up of its *individual* members : the extent to which these differences—particularly the differences in mental structure—are innate or due to environmental influences cannot as yet be precisely determined. Psychological research does, however, seem to have established that in adult life they are as a rule fairly firmly fixed. It follows that any mode of life which is directed towards the goal of mental health for all must provide for these variations. In such matters as food, dress, speech, work and play, the widespread emotional need to be accepted by one's group may, indeed, exercise a pull towards uniformity, though one which (contrary to what is often believed) is probably less strong at complex than at primitive levels of civilisation ; and in the contemporary world this is reinforced by factors of technical convenience. But the counter-pull towards variation adapted to individual taste and temperament is equally real, and must have equal recognition in any healthy mode of life.

Actually, if the system of moral values that I have projected wins acceptance, and its implications are scientifically explored, the kind of picture which will emerge from the contemporary world might perhaps be somewhat as follows. The existing division of cultures into fairly distinct local patterns is likely to become less marked, though environmental differences of climate and other ecological factors will prevent its entire disappearance : one does not wish to wear tweeds in the tropics. Localisation of culture will diminish, partly because of the obvious effects of the growing technical unification of the world, and partly because, as we have seen, the variations of local cultures do not appear to be closely correlated with biological differences between local sub-varieties of the human race. And with the disappearance of highly localised patterns we may expect a world-wide culture, recognising one system of moral values, and in the main one moral code, to give much greater scope for variations (in other than moral issues) as between such non-localised groups as artists, vegetarians or bureaucrats.

In approaching this world we have, however, to walk warily ; for we have to recognise what might be called both primary and secondary elements in mental health. The primary elements are absolutes, valid for all men at all times, and codes which violate them, such for instance as those which permit deceit and aggression to undermine essential security in personal relations, are plainly injurious. The secondary element, on the other hand, derives from the emotional need of the individual to conform to the custom of his group. Inability to conform, up to the point which this need demands, has been clearly established as a prominent factor in neurotic illness, and allowance must be made for this in the attempt to win acceptance for a common conception of human 'good'; whilst similar allowance must also be made (though this often raises most difficult practical issues) in judgments on individuals. The ritual murderer not only does not 'know any better': it is also true that if he did know better, he could not, without definite self-injury, ostracize himself from the community of which he is a member—quite apart from any specific penalties which that community may choose to impose upon him. That is the crux of the problem.

V

Finally, we have to meet the challenge that a secular system of morals has no reliable sanctions behind it: that it is, in fact, literally necessary to put the fear of God into people in order to make them behave properly. This view both over-estimates the strength of religious sanctions and under-estimates the psychological forces at work behind all moral sanctions, whether religious or not. It over-estimates the force of religious sanctions for reasons already given[1]; and the widespread recognition of moral standards in contemporary society by persons in whose lives religious belief plays no active part is some evidence of how much it under-estimates the force of sanctions that have no supernatural basis. Some Christians recognise this. 'The gospel of Humanism at its best offers a splendid conception of Man as he should be, and its sensitive exponents serve an ethical ideal with a devotion that shames nominal Christians'.[2]

The notion that the lowering of moral standards in the modern world is due to the decay of religious belief is an extremely superficial, not to say wishful, interpretation of highly complex

---

[1] See pp. 130 ff.
[2] *How Came our Faith* by W. A. L. Elmslie (Cambridge University Press), p. 373.

phenomena. In the supposed wickedness of our time, there are at least three major factors to be taken into account. The first is a conscious and considered change in moral codes, actions previously thought to be immoral being now admitted as moral by people who take their ethics seriously : this is most important in the realm of sexual morals. The second factor is the increasing technical power of the wicked. Hitler could do more far-reaching harm than Nero : it was not superior virtue that kept Nero from doing as much. Obviously, neither of these two factors is responsible for anything more than an *apparent* decline in respect for moral standards. The third factor—or perhaps one should say, group of factors—has caused a deterioration that is not merely apparent but real. It comprises all the dislocations that are due to the war ; the break-up of traditions, standards and settled habits ; the familiarity that millions have acquired with brutality and man-made suffering ; and, in all occupied countries, the deliberate inculcation of the duty to deceive and cheat all official authority. Those disintegrating blasts have assailed the moral standards of millions of ordinarily honest and kindly men and women, quite irrespective of their religious opinions.

Certainly the number of those who actively disbelieve in any deity, together with the far larger number who have never given the matter much serious thought at all, far exceeds the total of those who make no distinction between right and wrong. These last appear, indeed, to be only a tiny handful in any community. Nor can these facts be explained away by saying that in a professedly Christian society, non-Christians generally accept the moral standards of Christianity. If being moral depends on being a Christian, why should they accept any standards at all ? I have already argued that the *content* of secular moral codes is not simply plagiarised from Christian standards ; but even if it was, this would not explain why these codes exist—why the unbeliever, with no supernatural sanction behind him, should recognise any moral imperatives at all, whether he lives in a traditionally Christian community or not.

The answer is that for the religious and irreligious alike, the *practical* determinants of moral behaviour are much the same. These operate at different levels. At the more superficial level acceptance of moral standards is part of a general conformity with the way of life of the group of which we feel ourselves to be members. The discomfort of being peculiar is both deep and pervasive. It is a powerful determinant of behaviour in spheres which have nothing to do with morality, and in which nobody would think of invoking a divine sanction. On a hot day in London or New York there would be nothing inherently immoral or irreligious in attending a fashionable party in your bathing suit : and it would, indeed, be very comfortable to do so. But a convention which permits you to appear in a prescribed measure of undress upon a public bathing-beach forbids you to do the same in a city salon. The primary reason for observing this convention is exactly the same as the primary reason for accepting the moral standards of our friends and neighbours : in each case the motive is fear of that exclusion from the group which is the penalty of non-compliance.

In complex societies such as those of the contemporary Western world, it will, indeed, be found that, just as sub-groups within larger groups have each evolved their own variants of a more general pattern in the trivialities of behaviour, so also there are moral codes within codes. Within our own community an evening invitation demands formal dress in some circles, whilst in others this would be unheard of. Similarly, particular social groups tend to have their own peculiar standards of honesty, especially in their treatment of public, as distinct from individual, property. Although soldiers are only civilians in uniform, they often, as their fertile vocabulary of euphemistic words for stealing shows, have a rather different attitude in this matter from that generally respected in civilian life. In other cases standards seem to vary from locality to locality.[1] In this context it is significant also

---

[1] For further discussion of this subject, see my article on *Public and Private Honesty* in the *Political Quarterly*, July-September, 1945.

that it is nearly as uncomfortable to have a moral standard more exacting than that of one's neighbours as it is to have one that is less so. Fear of being thought a prig is simply one variety of fear of social rejection, but a fear so formidable that it sometimes leads individuals whose standards diverge *upwards* from those of the circle in which they chiefly move actually to conceal the fact that this is so. The primary moral sanction is the need to keep in step.

Even religious belief itself is largely accounted for by the same process. The vast majority of Christians or Muslims adhere to their particular faith because they live in a Christian or Muslim country, not because the evidence for the religion of their choice appears, after comparative study, to be more convincing than that on which any other is grounded. In short, most of us most of the time accept the way of life of our own community very much as a whole, alike in small things and in great. We keep in step because it is uncomfortable to be conspicuously different. The most religious person feels this social pressure just as much as the heathen. In so far as the moral code of a religious believer is in harmony with that of the community in which he lives, the path of virtue is made easy for him by the fact that it is clearly marked and well trodden by his neighbours: he does not, so to speak, have consciously to mobilise his religion every time that he chooses right instead of wrong. In so far as his code may run counter to the prevailing standard of morality, religious faith cannot obviate, though it may fortify him to face, the distress of social rejection.

In this lies the answer to the argument that an agnostic system of morals is all very well for an intellectually sophisticated minority, but hopelessly unreliable as an anchorage for the morals of the masses. Actually, the moral standards of any group are part of its general social tradition: the origins of that tradition as well as the processes which induce conformity to it are always complex. But we can at least say that the moral code of any community is necessarily supplied ready-made to most of its members most of the time. The fact that the Churches go to such pains to inculcate religious belief and the morality of which they approve shows that they cannot trust each of us to arrive at the truth through our private revelation : morals must be handed out, no less than charity. Religious and secular morals alike are, in fact, consciously elaborated by a minority and accepted through largely unconscious processes by the majority who have no call to be specialists in this matter. The only difference between them in this respect is that those who formulate religious codes of morality profess to speak in the name of God; and that, therefore, once the habit of conscious criticism spreads, such codes are credible only so long as this claim is credible ; whilst the secular moralist speaks in terms of simple consideration for common human needs, and is convincing just so far as the significance of these is recognised.

This interaction between the individual and his group even goes so far as actually to shape the structure of the individual personality to suit the particular pattern of his community. The closeness of this relation between individual character-structure and the norm approved by a particular culture has been much illuminated by recent anthropological research.[1] Close though this connection is, it is nevertheless a mistake to view the tendency to conform to type with alarm. For that tendency is an essential piece of social machinery. None of us, even at a very simple level of civilisation, still less in the complex societies of today, could face the demands of every-day life if we were not equipped with a good supply of ready-made conventions with which to meet all likely situations. Life is too short for us to make our own social and moral clothes. What matters is that the drive towards homogeneity should itself be directed by intelligent modification of accepted patterns from time to time in the light of new knowledge : the drive itself cannot be blocked without turning orderly social life into chaos.

At a deeper level, the peculiar sense of absoluteness attaching to moral imperatives is explained by a conditioning process on which modern psychological research has thrown much light. The

---

[1] See for example Ralph Linton's *Cultural Basis of Personality* (Routledge).

'absolute, categorical, and other-worldly quality of moral obligation, on which moral philosophers lay such stress ... is due in the first instance to the compulsive all-or-nothing mechanism by which the primitive super-ego operates'.[1] Conscience, it now appears, arises very early in life from the conflict between the infant's love for its mother (or mother-substitute) and its discovery that she is also the source of authority, frustrating some of its impulses. In this latter capacity the mother becomes the object of hate; but since she is also the loved one, a load of guilt attaches to the hate emotion, which must therefore be inhibited and repressed. In this primitive feeling of guilt, evoked at an age that none of us consciously remembers, is stored the motive force behind conscience. The whole 'proto-ethical mechanism', as Julian Huxley calls it, has the peculiar compelling force which we have learned to associate with emotions which have been largely repressed into the unconscious mind. It is, moreover, a mechanism that has close parallels in the physical field, in which, as Huxley points out,[2] at both the muscular level and the reflex level, a given impulse is accompanied by devices to inhibit conflicting impulses from coming into action. And the unconscious drive is in turn reinforced by the craving of the human mind for intellectual certainty in all fields.

This combination of guilt-feeling plus desire for rational explanation of the universe may account for the origin of religious belief itself. An external deity is invented to explain the otherwise unaccountable force attaching to the promptings of conscience. But the force of conscience itself is nevertheless derived from internal emotional experiences independent of any conscious hypothetical explanation in theological or other terms: it goads the godly and the ungodly alike. Psycho-analytic research has shown, moreover, that its strength in individual cases can often be quite directly related to the efficiency with which the infantile conditioning process has been carried out. The morbidly hyper-

---

[1] T. H. Huxley and Julian Huxley, *Evolution and Ethics* (Pilot Press), p. 109.
[2] *Op. cit.*, p. 108.

sensitive conscience turns out to be due to an excess load of guilt arising from exceptionally severe repression in infancy.

Conscience and ability to feel guilt are, of course, fashioned independently of the things that people feel guilty about—as witness the variety of actual ethical codes already remarked upon. The proper *content* of an ethical code is a matter to be intellectually explored by the usual processes of science, on the basis of ultimate moral hypotheses, such as the hypothesis suggested in this chapter that morality should be derived from an organism's biological need to fulfil itself. But it can now be said with some confidence that we know what makes conscientious, moral people who will respect whatever principles of right and wrong a particular code dictates.

None of this could happen, of course, if our minds were not such as to be amenable to the conscience-making process. To quote Julian Huxley again, 'the capacity . . . to *feel* the sense of rightness or wrongness', and 'the craving for certitude' are 'given from within, by the nature of the human mind', even if they are 'not completely determined by genetics, like the colour of our hair'.[1] Nature is to this extent on the side of the moralists. We cannot indeed, go so far as to argue that at any stage in human development the more moral individual has any certainly greater chance of survival and reproduction than has the less moral : there cannot have been any continuous and consistent selection in favour of those who are innately best adapted to the moral conditioning process. But capacity to recognise moral imperatives is essential to social organisation ; and social organisation in turn is essential for fashioning the enormously powerful weapons with which man masters his non-human environment as well as any human enemies. In our own day the advance of science could not have come about without widespread respect for complex moral systems, ranging from the belief that knowledge is good, to respect for our neighbour's life and property, including his laboratory. If, therefore, there have been any branches of the human

---

[1] *Op. cit.*, p. 177.

family in which the capacity for moral conditioning was generally absent or rudimentary, it is unlikely that they would have survived. We can take for granted that susceptibility to moral conditioning is now part of the normal character of the human mind as much as two eyes and a nose are part of the normal body ; even if in existing societies occasional individuals who appear to be completely amoral can and do survive and perpetuate themselves, under the protection (often very costly) of the moral majority. The number of such defectives is happily very small, and many psychologists appear to believe that their condition is generally due to the absence of normal relations with a mother or mother-substitute in early infancy. Possibly in some cases a genetic factor is also operative ; but on this important matter we must await the results of further research.

CHAPTER SEVEN

SCIENCE AND THE ARTS

I

THE question of the relationship of science to the arts clearly raises very much the same issues as the relation of science to religion and morals. Once more we are plunged into problems of value, and once more we meet the doctrine that art and science like religion and science are complementary, each interpreting a different aspect of experience : that the scientist reaches scientific truth by the familiar process of observation, hypothesis, verification, while the artist has a direct apprehension of artistic truth to which he then gives expression through the physical medium of his particular art. The artist does not indeed as a rule assert, like the theologian, that this apprehension is a direct revelation from God. At most he claims inspiration, but he is often no less firmly convinced than the theologian that his truth is reached by extra-scientific means. 'The creative element in works of art... is shown to be something which will always elude the analysis and measurement to which science by its method is committed'.[1] ...'irrational mental processes, akin to those by which works of art are experienced are also required to discover and appraise the values, to reach the ethical as well as the aesthetic judgments to which science so often appeals in considering the evolutionary process, but never explains or justifies.' 'It is my contention that the sense of importance we associate with works of art, with poetry and music, as well as with all disinterested scientific enquiry and the service of humanity, proceeds from a non-rational faculty ; and this may well be an organ by which we may penetrate to the

---

[1] *Science and the Creative Arts* by W. B. Honey (Faber), Preface.

truth of things more directly than in any other way'.[1] In short, to use Professor Ritchie's example again, we cannot ever lay down rules for 'writing poems like Shelley or making statues like Praxiteles'.

This theory is itself capable of two alternative interpretations, and is in fact used in two different senses. On the one hand, it may mean that the artist by his special insight reaches truths which are of the same nature as those discovered by science, truths which are, in fact, laws of association empirically valid, though the artist is hardly likely to put it that way. In this sense it is the artist's peculiar gift to make a short cut to scientific truth, and in that rôle he can be, as we shall see, a most valuable handmaid of science. Because, however, this aspect of the arts is generally ranked as secondary to their main function, I shall leave discussion of it[2] until after we have considered the alternative meaning of the theory that the artist has a special kind of truth of his own.

According to that alternative, the artist has something to say which cannot be translated into the language of science. Here again there is some danger of confusion. We have to distinguish between those cases in which the artist does, and those in which he does not, make statements which, whatever meaning he himself attaches to them, also fall within the field of science. When, for instance, he paints a completely non-representational picture he makes no such statements; but when he paints a picture in which a woman is shown with, say, a violin in place of one of her legs, he is unavoidably making statements in the province of anatomy. And when a work of art does contain propositions (which need not, of course, necessarily be verbal) that fall within the field of science, these propositions cannot be, in some mystical way, exempted from the necessity of being either true or false. Empirical observation quickly establishes that a woman does not have a violin in place of a leg: and we are, therefore, entitled to say that a picture which represents her in that way is anatomically false.

---
[1] *Ibid*, pp. 11, 13.
[2] See pp. 174 ff.

Actually, of course, the artist is not likely to deny this, for he is not so much concerned with a special kind of truth of his own as *indifferent to* the truths of science : indeed, he is quite prepared to tell scientific lies because he has more important things to talk about, and these may even be incompatible with respect for scientific truth. No matter that the anatomical details of his picture are incorrect : his job is not to give lessons in anatomy, but to paint an artistically meritorious picture. In other words, the theory that the artist has his own special brand of truth really means, as is implied by the word 'meritorious' in the preceding sentence, that he is concerned not, like the scientist, with empirical laws of association, but, like the moralist, with values. The artist has no need to trouble his head about the scientific accuracy of his work ; but he must be concerned that whatever he has to say, in language or in music, on canvas or in stone, shall be well, and not badly, said by the standards of his art.

On that, however, obviously no pronouncement can be made unless we know what those standards are : and since that knowledge involves a judgment of value, we must admit straight away that this, like our ultimate moral judgments, is not a matter on which science can speak with authority. Once more, however, if the scientist must suspend judgment, he can at least console himself that everybody else must do the same ; for theories of artistic value must pay the usual price in terms of perennial uncertainty for the perennial youth which they share with other metaphysical disputations. Similarly, of course, without some accepted criterion of artistic merit, there can be no progress in artistic achievement parallel to the characteristic progress of science. Brilliant though da Vinci's engineering may have been, jobs that the modern engineer can tackle would have been beyond him ; but Augustus John hardly enjoys a corresponding advantage over da Vinci as a painter. Indeed, theories of artistic value are not merely non-progressive : they all too easily degenerate into wholly circular arguments. Artistic merit must be measured, if the result is to have any meaning, in terms of some criterion external to itself ; but the problem is to find a measuring rod of which this is true, and to avoid the pitfall of measuring artistic quality by, say, aesthetic satisfaction, without implicitly defining aesthetic satisfaction as the emotion evoked by works of high artistic merit.

Nevertheless, as in the parallel question of moral values, to say that science is compelled to suspend judgment does not mean that all solutions of this problem are equally in harmony with a scientific outlook. In particular, the psycho-biological interpretation of human behaviour which sees this as directed towards 'the biological ends of self-maintenance, development or reproduction' or towards 'the normal completion or actualisation of the organism' will be inclined to include artistic activity amongst these goals. Empirical observation shows, indeed, that artistic activity or enjoyment in some form or other is widespread amongst human beings in all ages and climates. They sing, they dance, they paint, they make musical instruments, they write and act plays. It would seem that these activities must satisfy some fundamental human need : that, in terms of the criterion used in the preceding chapter, they are elements necessary to the mental health of the normal human organism. In that case, provided that we are satisfied as to the empirical objectivity of the concept of mental health (but on that condition alone), artistic, just as much as moral, values may be measured by this standard : and art is good in proportion as it contributes successfully to the mental development and health of the human organism.

This in turn raises the question, as in the case of morals, whether we can recognise any common standards of artistic value, or whether these are determined merely by the subjective needs of each individual organism : whether, in short, if you like jazz, I like Strauss, and our neighbour likes Purcell, there is any way of assessing the merits of our respective tastes. For if, in fact, no such standards exist, then all aesthetic theories are reduced to futile and irrelevant chatter ; just as are ethical theories if morality consists only of personal preferences. In the case of morals, it will be recalled, the weight of evidence did seem to suggest some common 'moral truth or standard' after which we were all fumbling. In the case of art much, but not all, of the evidence points in the same direction.

To take first the similarities: any theory which derives artistic standards from an anthropocentric view of the universe is as foreign to a scientific outlook as is its counterpart in the sphere of morality. There is, indeed, a difference, inasmuch as morality is mainly concerned with the relation of human beings to one another, while the arts are more often interested in man's relation to his physical environment. Nevertheless, though we may delight to look at the sunset and perhaps to paint it, yet if we are accustomed to rely upon scientific evidence, we do not delude ourselves into the belief that the sun sets the way it does for our particular pleasure. The arts, like morality, are a 'private joke of the human species'.

Again, we find something of the same variety of artistic as of moral standards in different communities. The Victorians and the classical Greeks had quite opposite opinions about the sinfulness of homosexuality: the works of art which they produced and admired were hardly less divergent. And just as there are always individual deviants from the moral codes of any community, so also individual artists have private codes or heresies of their own: Henry Moore's sculptures are not always acceptable to every President of the Royal Academy. Indeed, the scope of individual variation—at least in relatively sophisticated communities—tends to be greater, and the force of convention less powerful, in the case of the arts than in moral questions, if only because the penalties of nonconformity are generally less severe. Nevertheless, artistic heresy can provoke strongly hostile feeling: Epstein's statue of Rima was defaced when it was first placed in Hyde Park.

Here we touch upon a possibly significant point of difference between aesthetic and moral values. Morality, just because it is concerned, as has been said, with the relation of one human being to another, is social in a sense which is not necessarily true of the arts. One man's cruelty and aggressiveness is clearly a direct threat to the 'completion and actualisation' of another man's being; and moral values are, therefore, necessary to inhibit cruelty and other anti-social forms of behaviour. It is not so clear that one man's 'bad' taste need disturb anyone but himself; and if it does, the issue is moral rather than artistic. The question, for instance, whether a city architect should erect buildings which are repugnant to the local citizens may raise moral issues, but it throws no light on the relative merits of the architect's or the citizens' artistic standards. From this angle there seems to be no obvious reason why we should recognise any criterion of artistic merit other than the personal preference of the individual.

In the present state of knowledge, therefore, even on the hypothesis that aesthetic satisfaction is an element in the full development of the normal human organism, we cannot confidently say how far this entitles us to despise the taste of the Victorians or to label Chinese music cacophonous. It is on the whole easier to be confident about our right to deprecate ritual murder. Perhaps in the end the answer may prove to be that the whole mental (including the artistic) development of the human organism can reach different levels of complexity associated with more or less elaborate patterns of physical events in the brain; and that the 'higher' levels of artistic achievement or appreciation after which we struggle are those associated with the more complex of these patterns. But that is speculation.

What is not speculation is the fact that, *given* any definite criterion of artistic merit, the problem of how this may be attained is entirely within the potential field of science. Suppose, for instance, that great art is arbitrarily defined as work 'like' that of Beethoven or Bach or Giorgione, or any other list of artists to whom high rank is commonly accorded. The problem of producing great art then becomes strictly parallel to that of producing great science, on which something has already been said.[1] A repeat order for a Bach or a Beethoven differs in fact only from a requisition for a new Pasteur in the lack of precision in the terms of reference. The criterion of success in science is not in dispute.

---

[1] See pp. 14, 15.

The scientist's task is to establish by observation, hypothesis and empirical verification more and more comprehensive laws of association between phenomena : the more comprehensive his generalisation, the greater is his achievement. Once a similar criterion for determining success in art has been agreed, this difference disappears.

If, for instance, we decide to use for this purpose the standard just suggested, and to define great art as work comparable to that of certain arbitrarily selected artists, three lines of research suggest themselves. The first aims to resolve the meaning of the word 'like' in terms of the impact of a work of art upon those by whom it is appreciated. What, in fact, happens in the mind of the observer when he hears, say, the B Minor Mass, and judges it to be a great work of art ? At one level this is a psychological problem : it involves enquiry into the primary psychological experiences of the observer, as verbally communicated by himself, as well as measurement of his responses to other works, not included in the list of those already labelled 'great' for the purpose of our measuring rod. The technique of such measurement is similar to that used for any other problems in measuring differences between quantitative judgments as, for instance, in the measurements of the intensity of opinion already described.[1] At a more advanced level, this line of research may become physiological as well as psychological, involving enquiry into any physical changes taking place in the brain or elsewhere in the body which are associated with the contemplation of great works of art. If a man can already be made to see a particular mental image by the application of electric currents to the brain,[2] there seems no reason why associations should not, in due course, be established between the aesthetic emotion stimulated by a work of art and physical happenings in the body of the beholder. In that event, we should ultimately be able to define a work of art in terms of the physical reactions thus produced.

---

[1] See pp. 39, 40.
[2] *The Physical Basis of Mind* by Sir Charles Sherrington, O.M., *The Listener*, 5th May, 1949.

The second relevant line of research relates to the physical properties of works of art themselves. All such works are physical objects ultimately composed of sensory data—words, musical notes, shapes, colours, bodily movements on the stage; and all these properties are capable of exact measurements. From such measurements we may hope in time to detect relationships between these elements and the artistic quality of the result, judged by whatever criterion we may have selected. Even the touch of Schnabel's fingers upon the keys of a piano is a physical phenomenon: a sufficiently fine recording instrument could measure in physical terms the exact strength and duration of the force applied at every second. Such a record, compared with similar recordings of the performances by other artists, would reveal in precise physical terms the exact difference between Schnabel and the others. In this connection researches such as those of Mr. Udny Yule[1] into the statistical properties of certain authors' vocabularies may be of great pioneering value, in spite of their forbidding appearance.

Thirdly, the personal qualities of the artist himself, as well as any environmental factors which conduce to his activity, are themselves subjects for scientific examination. To invent techniques for the measurement of artistic ability is a task which differs only in degree from that of constructing methods for the measurement of general intelligence. And the extent to which abilities are determined by heredity, or dependent upon a favourable environment, is a field which science has already begun to explore, as also are the laws controlling the inheritance of specific mental qualities. Equally we may hope that the physical events occurring in the brain of the artist may eventually be examined, and correlated with his achievements, in the same way as the corresponding occurrences in the brains of those to whom his work is a source of delight. All these are, indeed, matters well beyond the limits of our present knowledge: but science has already touched the fringes of them all; and it is no more reasonable to treat them as

---

[1] in *The Statistical Study of Literary Vocabulary* (Cambridge University Press).

inherently inexplicable, than it would have been to write off the search for a scientific explanation of an eclipse of the sun, on the ground that manifestations of divine displeasure must necessarily be beyond the reach of science.

II

Such scientific exploration of every aspect of artistic experience puts the distinction commonly drawn between technical competence and artistic merit into a new perspective. It is generally accepted that it is within the capacity of science to contribute to technical accomplishment, in the sense of the artist's mastery of whatever physical medium is the vehicle of his expression. Nearly all artists seek to improve their own personal technique in order to express themselves more effectively, and they do so by the strictly scientific process of observation, hypothesis and empirical verification. The painter experiments with different strokes of the brush, the pianist varies his touch upon the keys, the poet tries different metres, or perhaps no metre at all. Each experiment represents an hypothesis submitted in accordance with the normal routine of scientific procedure to the test of experience; and in time the discoveries thus individually made mostly become common property. Further, the progress of scientific knowledge continually adds to the variety and subtlety of the technical instruments which are at the artist's disposal. The modern piano can produce a sustained sound on a single note which the harpsichord could not: the dramatist can write for television or radio as well as for the stage audience; and the film producer can appeal to both eye and ear instead of to the eye alone. The volume of technical knowledge, in fact, in the arts as in science, increases steadily through time. On that there is no dispute.

It is equally common ground that what is generally called technical competence, as Edith Cavell said of patriotism, is not enough. If it was, we should see similar progress in artistic achievement, and Italian primitives would be as obsolete as pre-quantum physics. But so far, indeed, is the artist from identifying technical accomplishment with artistic merit that he often deliberately neglects the most recent technical devices in favour of more antiquated methods. The technique of draughtsmanship—in the sense of accurate representation of primary sense-perception—has improved since the Egyptians used to draw a full-face eye in a profile; but this does not prevent some contemporary artists from treating the more precise modern method of representation as irrelevant. Presumably, these artists could, if they wished, draw more accurately than the Egyptians: apparently, however, they do not wish to do so.

But while it is essential to distinguish between technical competence and artistic skill, this does not justify investing the latter with a peculiar *mystique* as being a matter necessarily outside the field of scientific enquiry. And that would still be true even if research along the lines suggested should prove persistently fruitless. There is nothing unusual in that. Every map of research is studded with large empty deserts, where no results have yet been induced to grow. That normally indicates that the problems to be solved in those areas are exceptionally difficult or baffling; but the fainthearted inference that they are, therefore, inherently intractable by scientific method would have to be established in its own right.

Here, indeed, we touch upon the fundamental difference between scientific investigation into the factors that determine artistic merit (judged by any given criterion) and metaphysical speculations of the type discussed in Chapter V. The artist is dealing with physical objects, and his success or failure is measured (whatever criterion we may have chosen to employ) by the effects produced by his manipulation of these objects. The artist, his works, and (granted only that our criterion can be expressed in empirical and objective terms) the effects that he produces, can all be reduced to the primary sensory elements which are the raw material of science. Hypothetical laws of association about these elements are, therefore, subject to proof or disproof by the scientific methods in the usual way: a theory, for instance, that the arrangement of notes or rhythms in all great works of music corresponds to certain mathematical formulae could be immediately referred for empirical confirmation. Even the imaginative insight and sensibility characteristic of the great artist (and of the great scientist) are after all only problems in applied biology and psychology strictly parallel to the problems with which those sciences are already occupied. The artist produces pictures, the schizophrenic exhibits symptoms : and the study of either of these characteristic forms of behaviour is not *different in kind* from the study of the other.

Given time then, and the use of methods at once more refined and more rigorous than those now generally used, we may reasonably hope to see the arts yield up many of their secrets to science. In this prospect there is nothing to regret, and indeed everything to welcome ; for mystery begins only where understanding ends, and is, indeed, no more than a poetical name for ignorance. There is no virtue in remaining ignorant about matters which we might more fully understand ; for every time that man adds to his knowledge and understanding, he adds also to his dignity and his stature, and becomes more the master, and less the creature, of his environment. In every sphere the explanation of phenomena is the first step towards their mastery. The more, therefore, that we are able to explain what makes great artists and great art, the better are our chances of being able to enjoy more of the delights which these bring. Certainly, if we could know more about making statues like those of Praxiteles, London and other great cities might be more agreeable places in which to live.

The lines of research suggested here are, moreover, only a logical development of artistic criticism as at present practised. Indeed, if they are unpleasing, the only rational alternative is to abandon criticism altogether : since if a job is worth attempting with a blunt tool it is plainly even more worth tackling with sharp ones. All criticism seeks in fact to 'explain' how the artist gets his effects, and to appraise his successes and failures : that is to say, it seeks to relate the way in which the artist treats his materials and the patterns of sound or form or colour which he creates to the artistic merit of the result. The tools employed for this purpose are, however, generally still crude. The gulf between science and the arts has long been very wide : few scientists, even those working in such relevant fields as psychology, have, at least until quite lately, crossed it in order to make a really systematic study of the aesthetic process. And the critics, on their side, have not always recognised the essentially scientific nature of their task and the rigorous procedures which this involves. Partly, no doubt, because the use of scientific method in aesthetic criticism is necessarily limited by a prior, and not strictly scientific, judgment of values about the yardstick on which artistic merit is to be measured, there are risks that value-judgments may not be distinguished as clearly as they ought to be from purely scientific hypotheses. The art critic is perhaps on the whole less scrupulous than the scientist in observing Darwin's rule of always making a specially careful note of any observations that run counter to the hypothesis on which he is working ; and less ready to appreciate that investigation of the methods by which artistic effects are achieved must, if it is to be fruitful, be as completely objective as enquiry into the breeding habits of the Colorado beetle. In consequence, aesthetic criticism tends to be descriptive and even subjective rather than precisely quantitative ; and the associations which it suggests —as for instance that between a given pattern of rhythms and a particular aesthetic effect—are seldom framed in terms of any general law. It is much as if we noticed that the symptoms of a particular disease were associated with a rise in the temperature of the patient, without, however, being able to make any general statements about the relationship between bodily health and temperature. Indeed, one is sometimes even left with the feeling that the critics would actually be distressed if their methods should be too successful in revealing the secrets of the artist's mysteries.

There may, however, be another, and more fundamental, reason why much discussion of the arts is curiously ineffective. That is to be found in our failure to distinguish clearly between having an experience and asking questions about that experience. Science notwithstanding, an experience itself remains distinct from such questions as : what produces that experience ? or what happens in the body or mind of the person who has it ? If, as is I think widely felt, what matters in the study of the arts is that the student should have aesthetic experience of the highest possible order, then questions about the nature of that experience, or about how to get it (either in general or in a particular instance) are clearly ancillary to this purpose. The place given to them must be determined in the light of their effectiveness for that purpose and for that alone. That, however, is where we run into trouble ; for the fact of the matter is that at present the amount of hard scientific knowledge that we possess on the nature or the causes of aesthetic experience is extremely small. With active co-operation between the arts and the sciences it may, indeed, soon become much larger ; but at the moment it is not only small, it is also scarcely progressive : seldom does a contribution to research in the arts make a definite, objective and lasting addition, solidly grounded in empirical fact, to our knowledge of how an aesthetic effect is produced or how it may be more widely or more intensely experienced. The weakness, therefore, of study, and particularly of teaching, in the arts is that we have so little to teach.[1]

The result is that discussion of aesthetic experience tends to become not an aid to, but a substitute for, the experience itself. The substitute may, indeed, incidentally include small doses of the authentic experience itself. In many arts study and teaching usually include a good deal of 'background' factual material : we learn about the life and times of the artist and so forth. Experience suggests that a wide range of factual knowledge about both human and material phenomena delights the imagination, quite apart from its possible contribution to previously unrecognised laws of association : its mere acquisition gives a pleasure comparable in a modest way with that of aesthetic enjoyment; though it is sometimes difficult to disentangle the pleasure derived from a piece of knowledge for its own sake from that which is due to the

---

[1] As also, though in a different way, of the teaching of sociology. See p. 30,

SCIENCE AND THE ARTS

help it may give in explaining or understanding something. The satisfaction of learning about, say, Napoleon seems, in short, to have some of the same self-sufficient quality as the satisfaction of basking in the Mediterranean sunshine, quite apart from any parallels that may be drawn between Napoleon and Hitler (or Napoleon and oneself), or any lessons in military strategy that may be derived from his career.

In general, however, criticism is not merely a substitute for aesthetic experience : it is a greatly inferior substitute. It is this substitution, due itself, as we have seen, to the pitifully small total of our relevant knowledge, which is responsible more than anything else for the perversion of the study of literature into what Stephen Potter has superbly stigmatised as courses in Eng. Lit.[1] The problem is perhaps specially acute in literary studies because in these the alternative road by which the student can enjoy aesthetic experience—that of his own attempts at creativeness—is, for reasons that are not altogether clear, little used. That is less true in the other arts : the serious student of music, even if he is not expected to compose, must always himself play or sing, and the art schools normally require the student of painting or sculpture to paint or sculpt. But the production of original plays, poems or other imaginative works, as distinct from critical essays, plays a much smaller part in the typical course on English Literature. Something, therefore, has to be done to cover the nakedness of the land ; and too often a mixture of arid scholarship and banal criticism is the best that we have been able to think up. These lamentable tendencies are, moreover, as has often been remarked, in turn aggravated by the blight spread through the search for higher degrees—an infection which, by an ironic perversion, is itself largely due to the prestige of science. Since in the sciences it is only by research that we can advance the frontiers of knowledge step by step into the still vast territories of the unknown, the standing of the arts too often compels them to copy this technique, even if many of the contributions to knowledge thus made are of

---
[1] *The Muse in Chains* by Stephen Potter (Cape).

little significance, in the sense that they provide the answers to questions which, apart from these peculiar academic urgencies, no one would have thought of asking. In the result one is sometimes tempted to think that, if aesthetic experience is the primary purpose of the study of the arts, it would be better frankly to admit how little any of us has to teach, and simply to furnish those who wish to learn with a list of the works from which aesthetic experience may be derived, and leave them to do the rest for themselves.

When all is said, however, we may take heart from the fact that these are only the troubles of infancy, for the ineffectiveness of much artistic criticism is plainly due to the weakness of its scientific backbone : and that is a defect which time and exercise in scientific method can remedy.

III

It remains to consider the ancillary function of the artist as discoverer or disseminator of truths which are strictly scientific. Since science normally expresses its findings in the language of either words or numbers, it is naturally those arts which also use this medium, that is to say, literature and drama, which are most conspicuous in this rôle. The artist, like the scientist, may make successful hypotheses about empirical phenomena ; and since many artists are exceptionally precise observers of human action, this is particularly likely to happen in the field of psychology.

The data which the poets and dramatists use are, indeed, often familiar enough—drawn from experiences of everyday life which are within the reach of everyone. But the artist's eye catches significant details which escape the clumsier observations of the rest of us ; and from these he builds an hypothesis in exactly the same way as the scientist, using no doubt, as has already been suggested, similar mental processes. These hypotheses are, however, then presented not in the exact and general terms used by the scientist, but through the imaginative presentation of a particular instance. *Hamlet*, for instance, is a psychological thesis quite apart from its capacity to evoke or to satisfy aesthetic emotion.

It follows, of course, that the contribution which a work of art thus incidentally makes to any of the social sciences must be assessed in exactly the same way as the hypotheses of the social scientists themselves. If Shakespeare seeks in *Hamlet* to add to our knowledge of psychology, the extent of his addition will depend upon how far he has used the scientific method correctly, that is to say, both upon the accuracy with which he has observed his data, and upon the measure in which the inferences drawn from those data are confirmed by empirical experience. From the unusually acute observations of association between temperament, circumstances and behaviour embodied in *Hamlet* something may be learned about the feelings and behaviour of other people in like circumstances. But if the psychological hypothesis expressed in Hamlet's character was completely wrong, or if Hamlet's mental processes were wholly unlike those of any other person, nothing could be learned from the play, since scientific knowledge consists of general laws of association which enable us to argue from one event to another in similar circumstances : the kettle boils every day, not merely on the 31st July. Even so, of course, *Hamlet* might still be enjoyed, and, at least under some definitions of aesthetic value, it could still be judged as of high artistic rank, since discovery and artistic achievement are distinct processes : a play can succeed in one and fail in the others. But in estimating the contribution of *Hamlet* to psychological knowledge, it is perfectly proper for a psychologist to check the psychology of Hamlet against the findings of later psycho-analytic research ; and, in so far as these have brought to light knowledge that was not available at the time when the play was written, it is equally proper for the psychologist, on that point, though on that alone, to adopt towards its author the attitude which any contemporary physicist might assume towards Newton.

A work of art cannot, however, finally prove anything—except a hypothesis about works of art themselves. In that respect it differs from a scientific treatise. The treatise not only describes the data observed and suggests hypotheses about the association between these : it can also include a description of the empirical evidence in support or rebuttal of these hypotheses. Thus the hypothesis that rickets is due to a vitamin deficiency may be supported by comparisons between children who have, and children who have not, suffered such a deficiency, or by cases of sufferers who have recovered when the deficiency has been made good. These experiments can be described in the same work and the same kind of language as the actual hypothesis associating the disease with vitamin deficiency. But the thesis, implicit in *Hamlet*, that people's minds work as Hamlet's did can obviously only be supported by evidence from outside the play itself. The artist, in fact, can accomplish the first two, but not the third, of the stages necessary to complete the scientific process. He can observe, he can make an hypothesis, but for proof we must go elsewhere.

At the same time the form in which the artist expresses his hypothesis has peculiar advantages of its own ; and that is equally true when, as often happens, he is not so much adding to the total of scientific knowledge by putting forward a new theory, as disseminating, through his own special medium, knowledge which is already well established. There are many ways of learning ; and one of the most effective aids to grasping a general rule is the vivid presentation of a particular instance. The play and the novel, by the dramatic representation of particular characters or situations, are apt to impress upon us facts or generalisations about human behaviour or human feelings to which we might otherwise have given little attention. Some of Freud's theories are implicit in Ibsen ; and many will find that *Little Eyolf* leaves a sharper impression on the mind than do the *Introductory Lectures in Psycho-analysis*.

Few would, however, claim that it is a primary function of the arts either to add to the total of scientific knowledge or to popularise established scientific truths. *Paradise Lost* is not generally read for its merits as a serious treatise on cosmology. The primary interest of the artist is, in the ordinary case, to produce a work of high artistic merit : any other business is secondary. Nevertheless, his success in this principal rôle is closely intermingled with his effectiveness as teacher or discoverer. For it is the compelling aesthetic quality of great art which drives home any scientific lessons that the artist may have to teach : and, on the other hand, if the psychology of a play or novel is by scientific standards false, this is generally felt to react unfavourably on its aesthetic quality. Science and the arts are thus each simultaneously the servants of the other. While the scientist cannot finally settle the standards by which artistic merit should be judged, he can indicate that some views of this matter are nearer to the scientific outlook than others ; and, once the choice of criterion has been made, the whole field of artistic activity, and not merely technique in the narrow sense, is open for exploration by science. Conversely, while the discovery and promulgation of scientific truths is only incidental to the arts, yet the artist may reach new truths by processes entirely analogous to those of the scientist ; and he may present these discoveries with a force that many a scientist has cause to envy.

CHAPTER EIGHT

CONCLUSION

I

TO sum up an argument which has travelled a long way: the raw material of the social and the natural sciences is identical over a large area. Both are concerned with primary sense-experiences, but the social sciences also use comparable data from the world of psychological experience. Further, each of these two branches of science uses the same methods, formulating hypotheses which, after empirical verification, become laws of association between phenomena. Such associations do not always attain the rank of certainty even in the natural sciences: in both social and natural science the degree of their probability varies in different cases. This is, however, lower in social science as a whole than in natural science, though some of the observed associations in human affairs are more reliable than some of the associations recorded by the natural sciences. The social sciences are in particular handicapped by the difficulty of controlled experiment; but even in this respect their problems are not unique. About the nature of these associations nothing further need be said: science is satisfied if they can be shown to be consistently present: no theory of cause and effect, no 'invisible elastic', is necessary to explain them. In the social sciences this means that the question of freewill or determinism can be safely by-passed. We can predict that there will be crowds in Putney on boat-race day without being committed to the doctrine that people are not free to choose whether they will go to see the race or not.

The natural sciences are progressive: earlier work—however brilliant in its day—is revised in the light of later knowledge.

CONCLUSION

Among the social sciences also, those that are farthest advanced can now begin to see their own past in a similar perspective ; but the embryonic state of much social enquiry is betrayed by its inability to emancipate itself from the shackles of the past. Further, the progress of the natural sciences is everywhere largely dependent upon their ability to use quantitative methods ; so perhaps it is significant that the social sciences, in their turn, are becoming quantitative-minded. Admittedly, the measurements which have to be made in social science involve difficult problems, and the yardsticks available are still generally quite crude ; but the fundamental techniques are the same as those used in natural science.

Neither the social nor the natural sciences can make much headway in a hostile or superstitious environment. The natural sciences have had to fight hard battles and even to face persecution on this account ; and the dependence of the social sciences upon public co-operation and understanding is even more intimate. But, in the matter of any adequate appreciation of the scope and methods of the social sciences, most of us are still living in the dark ages. Moreover, many of our institutions are designed to perpetuate the pre-scientific mental climate of our age : party politics and press, as well as some of the concepts which dominate our education, all work to this end ; and so even more conspicuously do the dogmatic religious and political systems which we are expected to swallow blindfold.

All this makes it exceptionally important that the social sciences should not get off on the wrong foot : they have enough to do without that. There are, however, two lines of thought which seem to have a fatal fascination for students of social affairs. The first is that which regards human 'society' as a biological organism, in something more than a purely metaphorical sense—a notion which is equally incorrect whether a 'society' means a physical group of human beings, or a way of life. It is the peculiar danger of this doctrine that it serves as a pseudo-scientific cloak under which to smuggle its proponents' subjective valuation of the relative merits of various ways of life. The other brand of pseudo-scientific sociology is the travesty which Marxists have made of the hypotheses propounded by Marx—a perversion which is made the more tragic by the fact that Marx's theories were themselves well grounded in scientific observation and have made a lasting, though not, of course, all-embracing, addition to our knowledge. So long as the Marxist system maintains its hold, the contribution of every sociologist inside the Soviet Union—and of all too many elsewhere—is lost. Marx's theories can, moreover, be twisted to suggest that we are all so firmly imprisoned within the walls of our own age and place that no objective social science is possible, though naturally an exception to this gloomy generalisation has to be made in its own favour. Nevertheless, though we cannot be too careful about our own limitations, and though we must admit that as yet there are few laws in social science which can claim the universality of, say, the law of gravity, the case for such complete scepticism remains unconvincing.

The limitations of science are easily exaggerated. It is true that the scientist cannot find the answer to unanswerable questions about the ultimate nature of things; but, then, neither can anyone else. Science has, moreover, definitely disproved many of the doctrines which metaphysicians or theologians have advanced when they have been rash enough to wander into territories where empirical verification is possible—with the result that the metaphysicians must increasingly confine themselves to metaphors, while the Almighty threatens to dissolve into 'undifferentiated ooze.' The validity of revelation, again, cannot be either confirmed or refuted by scientific method; but it is indisputable that revelation—or more accurately revelations—lacks the consistency, the universality and the irresistibility characteristic of the data on which science is founded; and the scientist is entitled to demand that revelation should be treated at least with the scepticism which is the normal scientific attitude to all unproven hypotheses, as he is entitled equally to emphasise that scientific discovery has, to put the matter at its lowest, produced no evidence at all to confirm an anthropocentric view of the universe. And, in spite of the implied flattery, he is bound emphatically to reject the sophistical argument which attempts to clothe theological hairsplitting with the prestige of science.

The limitation expressed in the statement that while science can tell us how to do things, 'no science can tell us what to do' turns out to be not so simple as it looks; for everything depends on the point at which means end and ends begin. Somewhere an ultimate moral choice must be made on which science cannot pronounce authoritatively; but it makes a world of difference to the possible scope of social science whether this line is drawn at the point which decrees: 'Thou shalt not play tennis on Sunday', or 'Thou shalt not commit adultery', or 'Thou shalt honour the need of every human organism to persist in its own being and to reach its normal completion or actualisation'. The general effect of scientific research hitherto has been to push this line continually farther back, and so to enlarge the territory of science.

Science again cannot finally determine whether the various moral codes that humanity has evolved have more than a local and temporary significance; but the essential homogeneity of our species makes such an hypothesis look probable. On the other hand, the arguments for rejecting an anthropocentric view of the universe as a whole are equally damaging to the view which makes human morality a matter of divine concern. The scientist on that account is likely to look elsewhere, and particularly, since man is a biological organism, to concepts derived from biology, for his ultimate moral principle. That principle he may well find in the conception that for human beings the normal biological goal of self-maintenance, development and reproduction includes mental as well as physical elements, and that moral actions are those which enable human organisms to reach this goal. If he takes that view, he is not, as is sometimes suggested, merely stealing Christian morality, nor is he undermining the sanctions of moral behaviour. His moral code is likely to overlap with those of the Christian and other religions but not to coincide with any. Nor are the sanctions of Christian morality as powerful as they are sometimes made to appear : in the ordinary case they rest, indeed, upon belief in a remarkably improbable series of events. Actually, the forces which induce conformity to any moral code appear to be derived from practically universal social mechanisms that are operative in infancy.

The discoveries of the natural sciences brought them into violent conflict with religious dogmas. In these battles science was always victorious, though it is now fashionable for the churches to pretend that the disputes have been settled by mutual recognition of the sovereignty of science and religion each in its own appropriate sphere. This pretence had some substance so long as the churches were left with undisturbed authority on questions of morality or sin. Now, however, that the human sciences are beginning to challenge that authority also, the battle is likely to be renewed ; and the churches are faced with the alternative of either maintaining doctrines contested by science (a policy which in the past has always ended disastrously for them), or withdrawing their God so far into the cosmic background that he ceases to be in any meaningful sense accessible to the ordinary human being.

The co-operation of science and the arts is still lamentably rudimentary. It is true that, as with morality, science again cannot give the final word on the standard or standards by which aesthetic merit should be judged, though she may have hints to offer even on that. But given these standards, the whole field is open for scientific method to explore the psycho-physical processes involved in artistic creation and appreciation; and from such explorations we may expect the distinction—valid enough at the moment—between technique (which is progressive) and aesthetic distinction (which bloweth mysteriously where it listeth) to become blurred. In all this, however, the work of the scientist remains ancillary to, and is no substitute for, the aesthetic experience which the artist aims to produce. Moreover, the scientist, in his turn, is often deeply in the artist's debt ; for the artist, particu-

CONCLUSION

larly in literature and drama, may be an acute observer in the strictly scientific sense, and from his observations he, no less than the scientist, may draw valid and significant inferences about human behaviour. These he is likely to present with a vividness quite uncharacteristic of a scientific text-book.

II

This story suggests both certain morals to be drawn and some objections to be met.

The fundamental moral is, perhaps, that we should keep four distinct mental processes clear, not mistaking one for another, or asking any one to do a job which is beyond its competence. The first process is speculation, defined as asking questions to which we have no hope of getting generally convincing answers. Speculation, as we have seen, keeps the philosophers young; but it is irritating to those who think that the purpose of asking questions is to get answers to them. The second process is scientific enquiry. The peculiarity of this is that sooner or later it generally does get answers to the questions which it asks; and, what is more important, when those answers come—at least in the natural sciences—they command a unique practical respect from all and sundry. Philosophers may, indeed, dispute the theoretical standing of the laws of science, but they, like the rest of us, betray the hollowness of their doubts by their everyday actions. For these reasons the scientific method is entitled to rank as the only method by which we ever learn anything : by which, that is to say, we make solid additions to the growing heap of definitely established knowledge. Scientific enquiry is, however, limited by the nature of its primitive sensory and psychological data. Anyone who wishes to go beyond these must fall back on speculation and be content to do without answers to his questions.

The third process is aesthetic criticism. Strictly, this is only a branch of scientific enquiry, or at least an attempt at scientific enquiry; but, owing to the various muddles that have arisen, it is convenient to mention it separately. Finally, the fourth process, which must be classified as emotional rather than as scientific or intellectual, is aesthetic experience.

Confusion between the first two of these processes has bedevilled the development of a scientific sociology, and is responsible for the justice of such criticisms as that : 'The so-called social sciences encourage students to talk endlessly about alleged social problems. They do not seem to equip students with a single social skill that is usable in ordinary human situations. Sociology is highly developed, but mainly as an exercise in the acquisition of scholarship. Students are taught to write books about each other's books.'[1] Sociology, in fact, has got mixed up with speculation, and speculation deals with matters which cannot be referred for verification by primitive sensory or psychological experience. 'Argument, however rational, that is unrelated to a developing point of contact with the external world remains—however logical—a confusion of indeterminate possibilities'.[2] As I have tried to show, sociology or social science *is* properly related to such a point of contact with the external world, and its findings *can* be subject to empirical verification. By the use of scientific method, it can, therefore, if it will, qualify as a branch of science, and wholly disassociate itself from the philosophical speculations which have so unfortunately been its foster-parent ; and, on the commonsense assumption that sociology requires answers to the questions which it asks about human affairs, it *must* thus disassociate itself or else remain futile.

Confusion between the third and fourth process has bedevilled the study of the arts. As has, I hope, been sufficiently shown in the preceding chapter, aesthetic satisfaction is one thing : analysis of that experience or discussion of the techniques that produce it is another.

The long and the short of the matter is, therefore, that if we wish to learn anything, whether about art or literature or oceanography or alcoholism, we must use the observation-cum-hypo-

---

[1] Elton Mayo, *Social Problems of an Industrial Civilisation* (Kegan Paul), p. 19.
[2] *Ibid.*, p. 22.

CONCLUSION

thesis-cum-empirical confirmation method of science; but if we wish to enjoy ourselves, there are many ways of doing so, and amongst these (to suit all tastes) we must include both the pursuit of unanswerable speculations and the delights of artistic creation or the contemplation of beautiful sights or sounds. We find ourselves, in fact, in the position in which 'with no philosopher's short-cut to the mysteries of the Universe, we are left to gather what information we can about ourselves and the world by the patient and fallible methods of experimental science, and in the light of this information, freely to choose, each for himself, how he is to live . . . The now offered consolation of philosophy is no more than the knowledge that at least we have not anywhere deceived ourselves with high-sounding words; it is Montaigne's consolation; the maintenance of that tolerant and sceptical sanity which seems to survive the mutual destruction of the seekers for certainty'.[1]

Such a conclusion will undoubtedly be described (pejoratively) as materialistic. If a materialistic interpretation of the universe happens to be a true one, the label is, of course, redundant. Materialism is, however, such easy mud to sling that it is useful to be clear in what sense the description is apt. If a materialistic outlook means one which accepts as certain nothing that cannot finally be reduced to sensory experience, then the cap fits, except that the 'private data' of psychological experience have been treated as on a par with the evidence of the senses. Further, the attitude here suggested is, not only materialistic in this sense, but also frankly unspiritual in the sense that it sees no more evidence for the existence of a personal deity who is concerned for and in communion with the members of our own species, than for the reality of the furies who pursued Orestes, or the Loch Ness Monster. And, to complete this side of the account, it is a likely inference from what has been said, and from what we already know of the relationship of body and mind, that all our mental

---

[1] *The Development of Scepticism in Philosophy* by Stuart Hampshire, *The Listener*, 30th June, 1949, p. 1102.

or emotional experiences are associated with physical happenings in the body—though on this we cannot speak with certainty, and such an hypothesis is not essential to the basic argument of this book.

If, on the other hand, a materialistic attitude means one which assumes that man has no concern with anything above his belly, the description is altogether wide of the mark. For it is essential to the view here taken of the human organism that its 'normal actualisation' includes mental and emotional activities quite outside the range of any other species, and that the fulfilment of these needs is as much a part of man's nature as the satisfaction of his instinctive appetites for food and sexual satisfaction. Nothing that has been said in any way justifies exaltation of purely sensual satisfactions at the expense of intellectual, emotional or aesthetic experience, or detracts from the significance of such experience for our species.

Equally wide of the mark are the two related objections that any plea for a scientific approach to human relations overlooks—or indeed dishonours—the unique quality of every human being; and that it is not science that we lack, but love. Carried to its logical conclusion, the argument from uniqueness would rule out any kind of rational purpose in human relations. It is, indeed, plain that, just as every human being may be distinguished from every other by his physical appearance, so also no two personalities exactly repeat one another. Even identical twins are always exposed to at least slightly different environments and influenced accordingly. But unless some of the same elements recur in different situations, we should never have any experience upon which to draw for even the simplest social relationships. In the form that 'No two cases are alike', I have heard the argument from uniqueness used by organisations engaged in relief work as a reason for not keeping statistical records. Clearly, no two cases are alike in every particular, but neither are they in every respect different.

Indeed, the fact that those who are concerned with any

CONCLUSION

form of relief or personal service are all guided by some kind of principles, even if they do not work to actual rules, is implicit evidence that they acknowledge this truth. And the intimacies of daily domestic life rest, no less, upon the same assumption of recurring consistencies in human behaviour.

And if, indeed, it is love rather than wit that is lacking, the question is how to get it. Centuries of moral exhortation have not done very much. Yet even quite superficial observation shows that warmth and kindness and good nature seem to come more easily to some people than to others; and most of us would probably agree that if the character of every human being could be raised to the level of the most kindly and generous person of our own acquaintance, such of mankind's problems as are due to ill-will would be gone to-morrow. Surely then there could hardly be a more constructive line of research than that which would lead to discovery of the causes of these character-differences, for without that knowledge we are completely unable to move towards their elimination. And already something—a little more than nothing—is known about them, as, for instance, about the distressing character-changes that directly result from the physical effects of sleepy sickness, or the anti-social impulses induced by lack of affection in infancy. And the knowledge that we already have about such relatively extreme developments is at least a pointer to the quarters in which we might look for more comprehensive understanding. We shall not get love, any more than the moon, by crying for it.

Actually, of course, the theory that locates our social failures in the heart rather than the head is, like all apparently anti-intellectual doctrines, strictly intellectual in origin. Even the diagnosis that it is love that is lacking must, if it is to command respect, be reached by the scientific process of accurate observation leading to hypothesis: if the hypothesis is a mistaken inference, or the data have been incorrectly observed, the diagnosis will be wrong and the remedy will not work. Similarly, moral exhortation, and for that matter religious persecution also, is grounded in an implicit theory about the origins of virtuous behaviour : it is only the empirical verification which is deficient in this case.

Nor is it altogether wise to over-emphasise the responsibility for our misfortunes to be borne by positive ill-will, thankful though we should have cause to be, could we be rid of malice, hatred and all uncharitableness. For, unquestionably, one of the most tragic features of our present plight is the enormous wastage of ineffective or misdirected goodwill, both in individual and in collective relationships. Taken literally, the precept 'Do unto others as ye would they should do unto you' is most unfortunate advice : the non-smoker does not want a present of Havanas from his cigar-smoking friend. Love is, indeed, blind in more senses than one ; and it is arguable whether more unhappiness is caused in personal relationships by intentional unkindness than by the—purely intellectual—failure to convert kindly feelings into the practical form in which they achieve their intended result. This is equally true in both public and private affairs. The problem of the millions of ordinary peaceable men and women who find themselves plunged into wars for which they have no appetite is not primarily a matter of vicious intention ; and exhortations to love your enemies are hardly in place in circumstances in which the reward for doing so may be to get yourself hanged for high treason. Many—probably most—of these ordinary people are already quite prepared to love their enemies at least to the moderate degree to which they love one another ; and that, *given suitable social machinery*, is sufficient to enable the peace to be kept. At the level of the ordinary citizen, in short, the problem of war is not a problem of ends : his end is peace, but he lacks the means that will secure it.

The thesis that underlies my argument cannot, of course, be acceptable either to the Churches or to the Communists, for neither can face with equanimity the attitude which is prepared to follow the argument whithersoever it may lead : likewise, neither can tolerate the rival dogma promulgated by the other. In the Soviet-controlled regions of Europe, the battle between these rival

CONCLUSION

contestants for the human spirit now rages savagely, and the Communists, who have the advantage of exercising temporal power, are persecuting their enemies with a fury which rivals that of the Church in an earlier age. In the rest of Christendom, however, there are signs that the Churches are trying to turn this battle indirectly to account in order to discredit the scientific attitude which is really the common foe of both dogmas. Significant attempts are made to explain the rise of Communism as the result of indifference to Christianity, and to assume that the only choice before us is that between these two alternatives. Thus the Archbishop of York is reported to have told the York Rotary Club that Western civilisation and Marxian Communism were contending for the soul of man, and that 'we must make it plain that the fight is for man's freedom. The older boys and girls should be taught the value and the meaning of justice, truth, mercy and freedom, *based on Christianity*'[1]; Sir Stafford Cripps, again, is reported to have said at a Christian Action meeting at Blackburn that 'if one examines the comparison between Christianity and Communism there can be no doubt as to the falseness of the latter, but if we are to show up that falseness of this rival creed to Christianity, *it can only be upon the basis that we can make our Christianity an effective guide to our national and international life*'[2]: while the theologian Karl Barth has developed the same thesis.[3] The aim of these tactics is obvious: they are calculated both to belittle the significance of scientific anti-communist scepticism, and at the same time to win the support of its adherents in the fight against Communism.

To some sceptics such an alliance may seem unavoidable, at least for the limited objective of fighting the practical tyranny and intolerance which the Communists exercise whenever they wield the power of the State. The Churches at least have, in varying degrees, learned lessons of tolerance by which the Communists

---

[1] *Yorkshire Post*, 22nd January, 1949. (Italics mine.)
[2] *The Times*, 24th October, 1949. (Italics mine.)
[3] As for instance in his article on *The Church Between East and West* in *World Review*, July, 1949.

are still quite untouched, and in any case they are in no position to be otherwise than tolerably liberal in their attitude. Nevertheless the alliance is dangerous for the agnostic, since he may easily find himself manoeuvred into a false position. For, by diagnosing Communism as due to the breakdown of Christianity, the Churches are logically impelled to seize every opportunity that they can to spread their own doctrines : I have already referred to their success in making a daily 'act of worship' statutory in every state-aided school in England and Wales. The sceptic, therefore, who shares a common platform with the Churches in the fight against Communism would do well to make the terms on which he accepts that alliance unmistakably clear, and to leave no doubt about his complete rejection of both dogmas.

III

The proof of the social science pudding must be in the eating ; and that, of course, lies mostly in the future, for the greater part of the pudding is not yet cooked, and, as we have seen, the public are reluctant to taste the few morsels that are ready. Further, the ingredients are expensive ; and the social sciences have hitherto been much less liberally endowed with the public or private benefactions for research which provide those ingredients, than have at least the more advanced, the more conspicuously useful, or the more potentially destructive branches of natural science.

Money, however, begins to be forthcoming on a much more generous scale ; and, all in all, the established results of research in every branch of the human sciences now fill a substantial specialised literature of their own. Some of these researches already have been, and some look as if they soon would be, of real help in the solution of our immediate practical problems. The psychologists in particular have made large contributions, larger perhaps than has, as yet, any other branch of social science. Their work in vocational selection has, for instance, made possible the elimina-

CONCLUSION

tion of thousands of square pegs from round holes: recent advances in psychiatry have enlarged our understanding of the nature of the conditions for mental health, and of the treatment of mental illness: and much light has been thrown on the causes of crime and on the probable success of various methods of treatment.[1] In the long run perhaps one of the most significant of all the pieces of psychological enquiry of our day will prove to be the close investigation of the personality of Rudolf Hess,[2] which the happy accident of his flight to England made possible; for in this for the first time the psychiatrists, first of England, then later also of the United States, France and Russia were able intimately to observe the character-structure of a (till then) successful paranoiac tyrant, and its relation to the social environment of contemporary Germany; and, no less significantly, all these experts, including those from Russia, reached final agreement about the case. That, indeed, may have been the first step to full understanding of what makes the Hitlers and the Hess's of this world.

The ethnologists in their turn have wholly exposed the illusion that existing racial groups correspond at all closely to distinct biological stocks; and all the evidence that they and the psychologists together have so far collected supports a sceptical attitude as to the presence of significant innate mental differences between different races. The ground is thus cut from under the feet of the many cocksure myths about racial superiority; and the excuse for all the indignities and injustices which are inflicted in their name is destroyed. Meanwhile, the social anthropologists, by their exploration of the interactions of personality and culture, have illuminated the varying presuppositions of different moral codes—explaining incidentally how Japanese prisoners of war could give information to their captors without any sense of treachery, and how genuinely puzzled they were that English and

---

[1] In the United States 'prediction tables' have been drawn up by some investigators forecasting the probable future behaviour of persons appearing before the courts. See for instance *Juvenile Delinquents Grown Up* by Sheldon and Eleanor Glueck (Commonwealth Fund, New York), especially Chap. XII.

[2] See *The Case of Rudolf Hess* ed. by J. R. Rees (Heinemann).

American soldiers would not do the same in similar circumstances;[1] whilst nearer home the surveys of the sociologists make it possible to relate the structure and planning of new urban communities to the known needs of their inhabitants ; and the economists are hot on the trail of the scourge of unemployment and the trade cycle.

Of the fields still to be cultivated, one in which development is perhaps needed with particular urgency is that which lies in the borderland of politics (national and international) and psychology. The psychology of political life is still extremely crude : international politics too often reflect the psychological relationships of infancy, whilst on the national scale the reciprocal relations of politician and elector seem to be largely based on mental stereotypes. Little, too, is known of the psychology of the elector ; of the forces which make him politically indifferent or active, or a supporter of this or that party ; or of the measure in which his interest is directed towards shaping policy at the centre or taking part in its execution at the circumference. Even the distribution of power between the several organs of government changes under the involuntary pressure of circumstances, rather than in response to any informed conception of the requirements of sensitive and efficient government—and this in a generation when constitution after constitution in Europe and in Asia has been remade.

Certainly, the social sciences have their hands full ; but their achievements give ground for hope, and experience is on their side. The 'sordid and savage story of history has been written by man's irrationality, and the thin precarious crust of civilisation which has from time to time been built over the bloody mess has always been built by reason'.[2]

---

[1] See *The Chrysanthemum and the Sword* by Ruth Benedict (Houghton Mifflin, U.S.A.), especially p. 41.
[2] Leonard Woolf in *The Listener*, 9th June, 1949, p. 993.

INDEX

Ability, artistic, measurement of, 167
Absolutes, of religious morality, 132
Acquired characters, inheritance of, 100-1
Activity, directive, 136
Action, on partial knowledge, 60
Aesthetic experience, 172
Aesthetics, 6
Agnosticism, 97-8, 116
Aims, party, 59-60
Anthropocentrism, 118, 131
Anthropology, 2, 6, 12
  social, 91, 191
Argument, verbal, 52-3
Aristotle, 30, 88
Art, physical reactions to, 166
Arts, relation to sciences, 54-5
Asceticism, 145
Associations, 16-19
  in social sciences, 20 ff.
Astrology, 51, 107
Augustine, St., 95

Bacon, 15
Barnes, Rt. Rev. E. W., 101, 112
Barth, Karl, 189
Behaviour, indeterminacy in, 20-1
  recording of, 12
  and sense-experience, 8-9
Benedict, Ruth, 148, 192
Bentham, 70
Bias, in sampling, 50
Biology, 6
  analogies from, 72 ff.
  and moral standards, 134 ff.
Blood feud, 127

Bronowski, 18
Butler, Samuel, 21
Butterfield, Herbert, 117

Campbell, Norman R., 7, 15, 119-21
Cantril, Hadley, 39
Cartwright, 49
Category, meaning of, 105-7
Causation, 15, 18, 21
Christ, 99-100
Christianity, 87, 101-2, 118, 132
Civilisations and individuals, confusion, 73 ff.
Clapham Committee, 45
Class structure of society, 82-4
Cohen, Morris R., 33
Comfort, Alex, 129
Commons, House of, speeches, 56
Communism, 189-90
Communist Manifesto, 84, 86
Complexity of situations, 22-3, 24
Comprehensiveness, party claims to, 64
Comte, A., 2
Conferences, verbalism at, 56
Conscience, 157-8
Conscription, 121, 123
Conventions, 154, 156
Co-operation, limits of, 123
Creation, continuous, 112
Cripps, Sir Stafford, 189
Crises, economic, 83, 85
Criticism, art, 170
Cultural patterns, 148-9
Culture, unification of, 151
Cynicism, in politics, 61

Darlington, C. D., 54
Darwin, 87, 104
Data of science, homogeneity, 9
   of social sciences, 6
"Death" of societies, 73-4
Deduction, 19, 25-6
Defectives, moral, 159
Deism, 116
Demarcations, academic, 54-5, 80
Description, 11
   in social science, 45
Determinism, 21, 87
   self-contradictoriness of, 92
Discussion, 55
Distortions, in public thinking, 49
Dogma, 4
   religious, 65
Doubt, attitude to, 103-4
Durant, Henry, 39

Economics, 25-6
   and social life, 82-4
Education Act (1944), 65
Education, and social sciences, 54 ff.
Election forecasts, 38-9
Elector, psychology of, 192
Elmslie, W. H. L., 152
Emotion, 66
Ends and means, 59, 119-23, 181
Engels, F., 83
Ethics, 6
Ethnology, 191
Evolution, moral, 143
Experience, irresistibility of, 7, 9
   universality of, 7, 9, 124-5
Experiment and observation, 27

Fact, Press view of, 62
Faith, loss of, in social scientists, 117-18
Feibleman, James, 11, 124
Festinger, 49
Freud, 176
Friend, J. W., 11, 124

Garbett, Rt. Rev. C., 189
Generalisations, limited, 90
   unjustified, 49-50
Generic terms, use of, 80
Glueck, Eleanor, 191
God, change in relationship to, 112-13
   in metaphysics, 95
Guilt feelings, 157

Haldane, J. B. S., 87, 114
Hall, Bernard, 62
Hamlet, 174-6
Hampshire, Stuart, 185
Happiness, 139
Hardness, measurement of, 34
Harrisson, Tom, 45-6
Health, mental, 138 ff.
   mental and physical, as moral end, 137 ff.
   as unity, 140
   universal desire for, 140
Hegel, 82
Hell and heaven, 130
Hess, Rudolf, 191
History, 6
Honey, W. B., 160
   on Honesty, 154
Humanism, 65
Huxley, Julian, 157-8
Hypothesis, in art, 175-6
   formulation of, 14-15, 19-20
   testing of, 28

Ibsen, 176
Ignorance, and associations, 17
Income, distribution of, 85
Indeterminacy in behaviour, 20-1
Induction, 25-6
Inference, 12-13
In-group, 127
Insemination, artificial, 115
Institutions, and sense-experience, 8
Integrity, intellectual, 133-4
Intelligence, 141

INDEX

Intelligence tests, 35-7
Irresistibility of experience, 7, 9
Isms, 64-5

Japan, 76
Jeans, Sir James, 17
John, Augustus, 162

Keller, A. G., 78-9, 80
Keynes, Lord, 86

Labels, political, 63-4
Laboratory work, in social sciences, 24
Lasswell, H., 12
Laws, scientific, 15
  in social sciences, 20 ff.
Lay co-operation, 4-5
Libido, 26
Life-cycle of societies, 14
Limitations on scientific enquiry, 89
Linton, Ralph, 156
Literature, study of, 173
Lucretius, 88
Luis de Leon, 137
Lundberg, George A., 119, 120
Lysenko controversy, 60, 100

Malthus, 89
Marshall, T. H., 25
Marx, 72, 76, 82 ff.
  empiricism of, 82
  hypotheses of, 82-3
Marxism, 86 ff., 180
Materialism, 185-6
Matthews, Very Rev. W. R., 115, 122
Maugham, W. Somerset, 136
Mayo, Elton, 184
Meaning, 51
Measurement, 31-4
  in art, 167
  in social sciences, 34 ff.
Medicine, 6
Mendelism, 19, 110
Mercantilism, 89

Metaphorical theories, 19-20, 26-7
Metaphors, biological, 75-6
Metaphysics, lack of progress in, 93 ff.
  need of consistency with scientific progress, 94-5
Meteorology, 27
Middle class, 84
Mill, J. S., 70
Mind, development of, 137-8
Minds, open and closed, 108-10
Miracles, 99-101, 112
Moberly, Sir Walter, 97, 105, 109
Moral codes, religious and secular, 129
  unification of, 150-1
Morals, Christian, 122, 144-6, 153
  and man's development, 138
  practical determinants, 154
  progress in, 128
  religion and, 115
  science and, 119 ff., 181-2
  sexual, 145
  variation in standards, 125-6, 146 ff.

Nagel, E., 33
Nationalism, means not end, 121-2
Natural selection, 78, 143
Newspapers, see Press
Non-rational, the, in art, 160-1
Notation, in psychological tests, 37

Observation, 10-12, 23, 27-8
  in daily affairs, 68
Opinion, public, measurement of, 37-40
Organism, directive activity of, 136
Organisms, societies as, 72 ff.
Owen, Robert, 103

Parliament, 56-7
Parties, propaganda methods, 63
Party system, 58
Perry, Commodore, 76

Philosophies, political, 63-4
Plato, 89
"Points", measurement by, 40-1
Politics, psychology of, 192
Potter, Stephen, 173
Prayer, science and, 111
Press, the, 61-3
　Royal Commission on, 62-3
Prices, measurement by, 41-4
Probability, in natural sciences, 16
　in social sciences, 22-3, 25
Prohibitions, purpose of, 123
Propaganda, honesty in, 61
Prosperity, selection by, 80
Psychiatry, 114, 191
Psychological experiences, 9-10
Psychology, 6, 10
　and experiment, 24
　position among social sciences, 24
　relation with sociology, 81
Public, and social sciences, 48-9
Punishment, 66, 129-30
Purposes, science and, 119

Questionnaires, use of, 50

Racial groups, differences, 147-8, 191
Rational thought, and daily life, 69
Rationalisation, 66, 123
Real, the, 7
Recognition, public, 48-9
Recording, 11
Rees, J. R., 191
Religion, 4
　deanthropomorphisation of, 113
　and morals, 129 ff.
　and science, relation, 110 ff.
　and social sciences, 113-18
Religious dogmas, 65-6
Resistance to science, 67
Resurrection, Jesus', 100, 112
Revelation, 101-3
　as "category", 106-7
　progressive, 95, 129
　relation of science to, 99 ff.

Revelation, as source of knowledge, 101-3, 104
　variations in, 102-3
Richardson, Canon Alan, 101-2, 105-8
Ritchie, A. D., 6, 7, 15, 19, 25, 28, 93
Rome, Republic of, 77
Ross, Sir W. David, 127-8, 138
Rumour, 49
Russell, Bertrand, 9, 28
Russell, E. S., 136-8

Sampling, 38
　ignoring of principles, 49-50
Sanctions, of morality, 129-31, 152 ff.
Scepticism, justification of, 97-8
Schnabel, 167
Schools, religion in, 65, 190
Science, as unique foundation of knowledge, 95
Sciences, relation to arts, 54-5
Scientific enquiry, factors influencing direction of, 88
Scientific knowledge, progressive character, 28-9
　quantitative element, 30-1
Scientific method, use in daily life, 68
Scientific progress, stages, 6
Sense experience, 6-8, 28
Sense observation, and miracles, 100
Sexual morals, 145
Sheldon, 191
Sherrington, Sir Charles, 166
Social pressure, and morals, 154
Socialism, 121
Societies, organic view of, 72 ff.
Sociology, hypotheses in, 26
　and psychology, 81
Speeches, Parliamentary, 56
Spencer, Herbert, 30, 72
Spengler, O., 72-3
Standards in art, generality of, 163-4
　variety of, 164 ff.
　moral, *see* Morals

INDEX

State, national, and survival, 136
Statistical methods, use of, 46
Student and public, relations, 47
Sullivan, J. W. N., 33
Superstitition, 3, 4
Survival, morals and, 134 ff.
Systems, preconceived, 64-5

Technical equipment in art, growth of, 168
Temperature, measurement of, 32
Tensions, international, 2
Terman, Lewis, M., 36
Terminology, 13-14, 51
Thales, 94
Theology, as empirical science, 104-5, 107-8
  static nature of, 95
  teaching of, in Universities, 109-10
Theories, 19
Thomas Aquinas, St., 95
Toynbee, A. J., 72-6, 79
Truth, in art, 161-2
Two-party system, 58

Unconscious mental processes, 10
UNESCO, 2
Uniformities, difficulty of detection, 90-1
Universities, theology in, 109-10
U.S.S.R., 60, 87
Utilitarians, 69

Value in art, 162-3
Values, 124
  moral, 125
Variations, individual, 150-1
Verbal issues, 52
Verbalism in education, 55-6
Verification, 28
da Vinci, Leonardo, 162
Vocabulary, 13-14, 51
Vocational selection, 190-1

Wages, Iron Law of, 89
Wallas, Graham, 69
Warfare, and research, 47
"Willingness", in pricing, 42
Woolf, Leonard, 192

Yule, Udny, 167